TRANSLATION OF
FILM/VIDEO
TERMS INTO
JAPANESE

NIHONGOYAKU:
FUIRUMU/BIDEO
YOOGO

Compiled by:
Henshuusha:

VERNE CARLSON

TRANSLATION OF
FILM/VIDEO
TERMS INTO
JAPANESE

This is the fifth book of a series in the following languages:

Konohon wa kaki no kokugo shiriizu no dai go-banme ni atarimasu:

Book 1 - French   ISBN: 0-943288-00-2
Ikkan - Furansugo

Book 2 - German   ISBN: 0-943288-01-0
Nikan - Doitsugo

Book 3 - Italian ISBN: 0-943288-02-9
Sankan - Itariago

Book 4 - Spanish ISBN: 0-943288-03-8
Yonkan - Supeingo

Book 5 - Japanese ISBN: 0-943288-04-5
Gokan - Nihongo

Set of 5   ISBN: 0-943288-05-3

ISBN: 0-943288-04-5

1 2 3 4 5 6 7 8 9 10

Printed in the United States of America

A DOUBLE C C PUBLICATION

CC

CONTENTS

MOKUJI

ACKNOWLEDGEMENT

With more and more Producers dispatching crews to every corner of this small planet the need for a book such as this is evident. It concentrates on certain words and phrases common to the film and television industries throughout the Japanese-speaking world. When applied they can turn a crew stymied by a difference in language into a cohesive working group.

This book emerged from personal notes. Years ago, when working with a Japanese film crew whose language is translated here I began writing words and phrases heard most often in a workday so that I could better understand and be understood. It didn't take long to discover that, through consulting a cross-reference it was possible to easily and effectively communicate regardless of the language spoken. And get the work done.

Because my notes were incomplete I called on many friends for help. They readily responded when they understood what the project would accomplish.

Those who contributed their time and expertise to this series may not all speak the same language; what they do have in common however, is a high regard for their chosen profession and the people who work in it.

The contributors to this book and what they do, follows:

HAJIMENI

Chiisana chikyuu no hashibashi ni made prod-
uyuusaa ga satsueitai o hakenshiteiru. Kono hon
wa sonna hitobito ni fukaketsu no mono desu. Kono
hon wa nippon no eiga oyobi terebi sangyookai de
tsukawareteiru senmom yoogo o shuuroku shiteimasu. Kono hon ni tsukawareteiru yoogo o tsuka-
eba chigatta kotoba no naka de kutoo shiteiru
satsueitai o umaku matomete shigoto ga hakadoru
yooni dekimasu.

Kono hon o watakushi ga jibun de kotsukotsu
atsumeta memo ga botai to natte orimasu. Suunen
mae nippon no fuirumu kankeishatachi to shigoto
o shitakato ga arimashita. Ichi ichi watakushitachi no kotaba ga tsuuyaku ni notte tsutaerare
nakereba narimasendeshita. Sokode watakushi wa
shibashiba tsukawareru kotoba ya goku o kakito-
merukoto ni shimashita. Soosureba otagai ga
motto rikai dekiru to kangaeta karadesu. Soo
suru uchi ni kotoba ga hanase nakutemo kotoba o
kookan suru daki de ishi dentatsu ga umaku iku
yoo ni narimashita. Okage de shigoto wa dai-
seikoo shimashita.

Watakushi no wa memo fujuubun desunode mochi-
ron ooku no yuujintachi no tasuke o ukemashita.
Watakushi no keikaku ga donnani taisetsuna mono
ka sono wa yuujintachi wa yoku rikai shitekurete
yoku tetsudatte kuremashita.

Kono ichiren no shogoto no tame ni jikan to
chishiki o teikyoo shitekureta yuujintachi wa
zenin ga onaji kotoba o hanshimasen. Shikashi
kyootsuushite ieru koto wa sore zore no hitobito
ga sono senmonbunya de takuetsu shiteori genba
de genzai hataraite iru to iukotodesu.

Tsugi ni kono hon o kanseisuru ni atari gok-
yooryoku shite kudasatta katagata no ryakureki o
goshookai shimasu:

iv

Kenji Saotome graduated from Sophia University in Tokyo and joined CANON, INC in Japan. Later he transferred to CANON USA, INC in California. He is Marketing Manager of the Western Region.

Naoko Taniguchi was born in Kobe, Japan. A graduate of California State University Long Beach, she majored in Asian Studies and obtained a TESI certificate (Teaching English as a second language). She translates Japanese technical texts, video, and motion pictures into English.

Dr. Ingrid Aall is an Art Historian, Professor at California State University Long Beach. She has traveled and studied worldwide. Her expertise in more than five languages qualified her as an invaluable consultant on this series.

To them, my deepest appreciation

VERNE CARLSON

Saotome Kenji joochi daigaku (Tokyo) sotsugyoogo, CANON, INC. Tokyo nyuusha. Sonogo CANON USA, INC. Karuforunia ni tenkin to nari, hanbai narabi ni shijoo kaihatsu tantoo maneeja to shite katsuyaku.

Taniguchi Naoko Kobe shussin. Karuforunia shuuritsu daigaku rongu biichi sotsugyoo. Ajia kenkyuu o senkoo, daini gaikokugo kyooju shikaku shutoku. Eiga, bideo, gijutsu bunya no honyaku/tsuuyaku ni juuji.

Inguriddo Aaru bijutsu rekichika. Kariforunia Shooritsu Daigaku Roongu Biichi kijaaju. Kenkyoo no tame. Mizukasa sekai-ju o tanbo shi. Go-kakokugo shutoku. Sonogo sono bunya no konsarutanto toshite katsuyaku.

Fukai kansha no kimochi o komete,

BAAN KAARUSON

HOW TO USE THIS BOOK

This first edition contains 16 chapters. Each chapter is titled by a general category that relates to a specific area of production.

Each category is divided into two pages. The number at the left of the page indicates the beginning of a new word or phrase on that page. Example:

ENGLISH	JAPANESE
1. good	1. yoi
2. page	2. peeji
3. How do you say this word?	3. Kono tango wa nanto iimasu ka?
4. What is this?	4. Kore wa nan desu ka?

By finding a word or phrase in your own language it is simple enough to run a finger across the page to the corresponding word or phrase and then speak, or indicate, the information you are trying to convey.

Good luck!   Umaku ikukoto ukeaidesu!

Note: As with any work some terms will be left out, change with use, or be revised by adaptation to a new technology. Any reader so desiring to contribute corrections is most welcome to do so. However, individual contributions cannot be acknowledged due to the exigencies of production.

KONO HON NO TSUKAIKATA

Kono shohanbon wa 16 shoo yori natte orimasu. Kakushoo wa seizoo seisaku no senmon bunya goto ni wakerare hyoodai ga tsukerarete arimasu.

Kaku bunya wa ni-peeji ni watatte imasu. Kaku peeji no hidari no suuji wa tanni sono peeji ni aru atarashii kotoba aruiwa goku no hajimari o shimesudakedesu. Tatoeba:

EIGO	NIHONGO
1. good	1. yoi
2. page	2. peeji
3. How do	3. Kono tango wa
you say	nanto
this word?	iimasu ka?
4. What is	4. Kore wa
this?	nan desu ka?

Jikokugo de mazu kotoba aruiwa ku o mitsukete kudasai. Soshite tonari no peeji to onaji takasa no retsu made yubi de tadoreba soko ni tsutaeyoo to shiteiru kotoba aruiwa ku ga shimesarete arimasu. Ato wa goku kantan desu. Tada kuchi de sore o itte miruka, aite ni sore o shimeseba yoi dakedesu.

Good luck! Umaku ikukoto ukeaidesu!

Bikoo: Donna koto nimo atehamaru koto desu ga, shigoto ga susumu ni tsurete nanikashira wasurete itari shiyoojoo no henkoo ga attari, atarashii gijutsu no hakken de sarani ooyoo ga kawattari suru mono desu nanika okizuki no ten ga arimashitara gorenraku kudasai. Shikashinagara seihon o suru to iuukoto wa hijoo ni jikan no kakaru taihenna koto desunode minasama yori no gojogen nari teisei o suguniwa hanei dekimasen. Arakajime goryooshoo negaimasu.

PRONUNCIATION

VOWELS AND DIPHTHONGS

Note: This romanized text employs the Jorden modification of the long vowels (normally written ā, ē, ii, ō, ū), and are written here as aa, ee, ii, oo, uu, to eliminate misunderstanding in pronunciation. Example: the word <u>beru</u> (short vowel) means *bell*, but the word bēru (long vowel) means *veil*, and is written in this text <u>beeru</u>. In the "phonetics" then, an apostrophe (') between the vowels indicates it is held twice the length of a single vowel and <u>not</u> as two separate vowels.

a	(ah)	as in	*pa*
ai	(eye)	as the *i* in	*mine*
au	(ow)	as the *ow* in	*cow*
e	(eh)	as the *e* in	*yet*
ei	(ay)	as the *a* in	*pay*
i	(ee)	as in	*machine*
o	(oh)	as in	*solo*
oi	(oy)	as in	*toil*
ou	(oh)	as the *o* in	*hope*
u	(oo)	as the *oo* in	*boot*

Note: Sometimes, when the vowels *u* and *i* appear between, or after, certain consonants they are almost silent. What is required is a slight whisper on the letter (almost half a pronunciation). Thus, *sukiyaki* (often mispronounced: soo-kee-yah-kee) is more like s'k'yah'k; *sushi* is more like s'sh'ee, etc. If said quickly, the pronunciation will be more correct.

CONSONANTS

b, c, d, j, k, m, p, s, t, & z are pronounced the same as in English. There is <u>no</u> *l, q, v,* or *x* in Japanese.

ch	(ch)	as in *chop*
f	(fh)	halfway between *f* and an *h*
g	(guh)	as in *gobo*
n	(nuh)	as in *nut* when it precedes a vowel
n	(en)	as in *tend* when at the end of a word
r	(rd)	as the British *r* in *very* (almost a *d*)
w	(wuh)	as the *w* in *win* with the lips slack

NOTES

NOTES

PERSONNEL

Animal Handlers:

01. Animal Trainer:

  a.   dog

  b.   horse

  c.   wild

  d.   domestic

02. Wrangler (livestock)

03. Wrangler (horses)

Art Department:

04. Art Director

05. Assistant Art Director

06. Set Decorator

07. Scenic Artist

08. Draftsman

Doobutsu Shiiku In:
Doh'oh-boo-tsoo Shee'ee-koo Een:

01. Doobutsu Chookyo Shi:
    Doh'oh-boo-tsoo Choh'oh-k'yoh Shee:

   a.   inu
        ee-noo

   b.   uma
        oo-mah

   c.   yasei
        yah-say

   d.   hitoni nareta
        hee-toh-nee nah-reh-tah

02. Kachikuban
    Kah-chee-koo-bahn

03. Batei/Umaban
    Bah-tay/Oo-mah-bahn

Bijutsu Bu:
Bee-joo-tsoo Bu:

04. Bijutsu Shunin
    Bee-joo-tsoo Shoo-neen

05. Bijutsu Joshu
    Bee-joo-tsoo Joh-shoo

06. Butai Soochi Shunin
    Boo-tye Soh'oh-chee Shoo-neen

07. Butai Soochi Bijutsu
    Boo-tye Soh'oh-chee Bee-joo-tsoo

08. Shitaekaki
    Shee-tah-eh-kah-kee

Camera:

09. Director of Photography

10. Camera Operator

11. 1st Assistant Photographer

12. 2nd Assistant Photographer

13. Film Loader

14. Cinematographer:

   a. aerial

   b. animation

   c. documentary

   d. newsreel

   e. process (rear or front)

   f. second unit

   g. special effects

   h. stop motion

Kamera:
Kah-meh-rah:

09. Kamera Shunin
    Kah-meh-rah Shoo-neen

10. Kameraman
    Kah-meh-rah-mahn

11. Dai-ichi Kamerajoshu
    Dye-ee-chee Kah-meh-rah-joh-shoo

12. Dai-ni Kamerajoshu
    Dye-nee Kah-meh-rah-joh-shoo

13. Fuirumu Sootensha
    Foo-ee-roo-moo Soh'oh-ten-shah

14. Eiga:
    Ay-gah:

   a. kuuchuu
       koo'oo-choo'oo

   b. animeeshon
       ah-nee-meh'eh-shohn

   c. dokyumentari
       dohk-yoo-mehn-tah-ree

   d. nyuusu eiga
       n'yoos ay-gah

   e. haikei setsugo (ushiro/mae
       hye-kay set-soo-goh (oo-shee-roh/mah-eh)

   f. yobi
       yoh-bee

   g. tokushu kooka
       toh-kee-shoo koh'oh-kah

   h. sutoppu mooshon
       s'tohp moh'oh-shohn

Camera (continued):

14. Cinematographer (continued):

 i.   underwater

15. Still Photographer

16. Projectionist

17. Cinetechnician (camera repair person)

Cast:

18. Actor

19. Actress

20. Featured Player

21. Supporting Player

22. Bit Player

23. Stand-in

24. Extra

25. Stunt Person

SHOKUSHUMEI (tsuzuku)
SHOH-KOO-SHOO-MAY (tsoo-zoo-koo)

Kamera (tsuzuku):
Kah-meh-rah (tsoo-zoo-koo):

14. Eiga (tsuzuku):
    Ay-gah (tsoo-zoo-koo):

  1.   suichuu
       soo-ee-choo'oo

15. Shashinka
    Shah-sheen-kah

16. Eisha Gishi
    Ay-shah Gee-shee

17. Kamera Shuurigishi
    Kah-meh-rah Shoo'oo-ree-gee-shee

Shutsuen Sha:
Shoo-tsoo-ehn Shah:

18. Haiyuu
    Hye-yoo'oo

19. Joyuu
    Joh-yoo'oo

20. Shuen
    Shoo-ehn

21. Joen
    Joh-ehn

22. Hayaku
    Hah-yah-koo

23. Sutandoin
    S'tahn-doh-een

24. Ekisutora
    Eh-kee-s'toh-rah

25. Sutantoman
    S'tahn-toh-mahn

Cast (continued):

26. Double

27. Man

28. Woman

29. Boy

30. Girl

31. Teacher

32. Welfare Worker

Directors:

33. Director

34. Dialogue Director

35. 1st Assistant Director

36. 2nd Assistant Director

37. Second Unit Director

38. Trainee

Shutsuen Sha (tsuzuku):
Shoo-tsoo-ehn Shah (tsoo-zoo-ku):

26. Daburu
    Dah-boo-roo

27. Otoko
    Oh-toh-koh

28. Onna
    Ohn-nah

29. Shoonen
    Shoo'oo-nehn

30. Shoojo
    Shoh'oh-joh

31. Sensei
    Sehn-say

32. Shakai Jigyooka
    Shah-kye Jee-g'yoh'oh-kah

Kantoku:
Kahn-toh-koo:

33. Kantoku
    Kahn-toh-koo

34. Kaiwa Enshutsu Kantoku
    Kye-wah Ehn-shoo-tsoo Kahn-toh-koo

35. Dai-ichi Jokantoku
    Dye-ee-chee Joh-kahn-toh-koo

36. Dai-ni Jokantoku
    Dye-nee Joh-kahn-toh-koo

37. Sekando Yunitto Kantoku
    Seh-kahn-doh Yoo-neet-toh Kahn-toh-koo

38. Renshuusei
    Rehn-shoo'oo-say

Editing:

39. Editor

40. 1st Assistant Editor

41. 2nd Assistant Editor

42. Sound Editor

43. Sound Effects Editor

44. Music Editor

45. Negative Cutter

46. Film Librarian

Electrical:

47. Gaffer

48. Assistant Gaffer

49. Best Boy

50. Best Girl

51 Electrician

Henshuu:
Hehn-shoo'oo:

39. Henshuusha
    Hehn-shoo'oo-shah

40. Dai-ichi Henshuu Joshu
    Dye-ee-chee Hehn-shoo'oo Joh-shoo

41. Dai-ni Henshuu Joshu
    Dye-nee Hehn-shoo'oo Joh-shoo

42. Onkyoo Hensshuusha
    Ohn-k'yoh'oh Hehn-shoo'oo-shah

43. Onkyoo Kooka Henshuusha
    Ohn-k'yoh'oh Koh'oh-kah Hehn-shoo'oo-shah

44. Ongaku Henshuusha
    Ohn-gah-koo Hehn-shoo'oo-shah

45. Nega Kattaa
    Neh-gah Kaht-tah'ah

46. Fuirumu Kanrisha
    Foo-ee-roo-moo Kahn-ree-shah

Denki:
Dehn-kee:

47. Denki Shunin
    Dehn-kee Shoo-neen

48. Denki Joshu
    Dehn-kee Joh-shoo

49. Jukurensha
    Joo-koo-rehn-shah

50. Jukurensha
    Joo-koo-rehn-shah

51. Denki Koo
    Dehn-kee Koh'oh

Electrical (continued):

52. Lamp Operator

53. Generator Operator

54. Cable Person

First Aid:

55. Doctor

56. Nurse

57. Paramedic

58. Attendant

Grip:

59. Key Grip

60. 1st Assistant Grip

61. Best Boy

62. Best Girl

63. Dolly Grip

Denki (tsuzuku):
Dehn-kee (tsoo-zoo-koo):

52. Ranpu Soosain
    Rahn-poo Soh'oh-syne

53. Hatsudenki Soosain
    Haht-soo-dehn-kee Soh'oh-syne

54. Keeburu Soosain
    Keh'eh-boo-roo Soh'oh-syne

Kyukyu Shochi:
K'yoo-k'yoo Shoh-chee:

55. Ishi
    Ee-shee

56. Kangofu
    Kahn-goh-foo

57. Junkangoshi
    Joon-kah-goh-shee

58. Iryoo Joshu
    Ee-r'yoh'oh Joh-shoo

Shoomei Kigu:
Shoh'oh-may Kee-goo:

59. Shoomei Shunin
    Shoh'oh-may Shoo-neen

60. Dai-ichi Shoomei Joshu
    Dye-ee-chee Shoh'oh-may Joh-shoo

61. Jukurensha
    Joo-koo-ren-shah

62. Jukurensha
    Joo-koo-ren-shah

63. Daishayoo Shoomei Kigu
    Dye-shah-yoh'oh Shoh'oh-may Kee-goo

Grip (continued):

64. Crane Operator

65. Grip

66. Boom Operator

67. Rigger

Makeup:

68. Key Makeup Artist

69. Assistant Makeup Artist

70. Body Makeup Artist

71. Key Hairdresser

72. Hairdresser

73. Appliance Technician

Management:

74. Executive Producer

75. Producer

SHOKUSHUMEI (tsuzuku)
SHOH-KOO-SHOO-MAY (tsoo-zoo-koo)

Shoomei Kigu (tsuzuku):
Shoh'oh-may Kee-goo (tsoo-zoo-koo):

64. Kureen Soosain
Koo-reh'ehn Soh'oh-syne

65. Shoomeikigu
Shoh'oh-may-kee-goo

66. Buumu Soosain
Boo'oom Soh'oh-syne

67. Hoshuu Yooin
Hoh-shoo Yoh-oy-een

Meiku Appu:
May-kahp:

68. Meikuappu Shunin
May-kahp Shoo-neen

69. Meikuappu Joshu
May-kahp Joh-shoo

70. Bodiimeikuappu
Boh-dee'ee-may-kahp

71. Heaasutairu Shunin
Heh-ah'ah-s'tye-roo Shoo-neen

72. Heaa Doressaa
Heh-ah'ah Doh-rehs-sah'ah

73. Setsubigishi
Seht-soo-bee-gee-shee

Keiei:
Kay-ay:

74. Seisaku Buchoo
Say-sah-koo Boo-choh'oh

75. Seisakusha/Purojuusaa
Say-sahk'shah/P'roh-joo'oo-sah'ah

Management (continued):

76. Associate Producer

77. Production Manager

78. Unit Manager

79. Attorney

80. Publicist

81. Location Auditor

82. Accountant

83. Bookkeeper

84. Production Assistant

85. Secretary

Properties:

86. Property Master

87. Asistant Property Master

88. Greens Person

Keiei (tsuzuku):
Kay-ay (tsoo-zoo-koo):

76. Seisaku Joshu
    Say-sah-koo Joh-shoo

77. Seisaku Shunin
    Say-sah-koo Shoo-neen

78. Yunitto Maneejaa
    Yoo-neet-toh Mah-neh'eh-jah'ah

79. Bengoshi
    Behn-goh-shee

80. Shinbungakari/Sendenjoohoo Gakari
    Sheen-boon-gah-kah-ree/Sehn-dehn-joh'oh-
    hoh'oh Gah-kah-ree

81. Rokeeshon Kaikeigakari
    Roh-keh'eh-shohn Kye-kay-gah-kah-ree

82. Kaikeishi
    Kye-kay-shee

83. Bukkukiipaa/Choobo Gakari
    Boo'k-koo-kee'ee-pah'ah/Choh'oh Gah-kah-
    ree

84. Produkushon Joshu
    Proh-doo-koo-shohn Joh-shoo

85. Hisho
    Hee-shoh

Kodoogu:
Koh-doh'oh-goo:

86. Kodoogu Shunin
    Koh-doh'oh-goo Shoo-neen

87. Kodoogu Joshu
    Koh-doh'oh-goo Joh-shoo

88. Shokubutsu Gakari
    Shoh-koo-boo-tsoo Gah-kah-ree

Security:

89. Chief

90. Captain

91. Lieutenant

92. Inspector

93. Sergeant

94. Guard

95. Armed Guard

96. Police Officer

97. Special Officer

98. Motorcycle Officer

99. Vehicle Officer

100. Traffic Control Person

101. Police Escort

102. Military Escort

Hoan:
Hoh-ahn:

89. Hoan Shunin
    Hoh-ahn Shoo-neen

90. Keibu
    Kay-boo

91. Keibuho
    Lay-boo-hoh

92. Keibu
    Kay-boo

93. Junsa Buchoo
    Joon-sah Boo-choh'oh

94. Gaadoman
    Gah'ah-doh-mahn

95. Busoo Gaadoman
    Boo-soh'oh Gah'ah-doh-mahn

96. Keikan
    Kay-kahn

97. Tokubetsu Keikan
    Toh-koo-beh-tsoo Kay-kahn

98. Ootobai Keikan
    Oh'oh-toh-bye Kay-kahn

99. Patokaa Keikan
    Pah-toh-kah'ah Kay-kahn

100. Kootsuu Seiri
     Koh'oh-tsoo Say-ree

101. Keisatsu no Goei
     Kay-sah-tsoo noh Goh-ay

101. Guntai no Goei
     Goon-tye noh Goh-ay

Security (continued):

103. Soldier

104. Sailor

105. Marine

106. Coast Guard

107. Firefighter

Set Construction:

108. Supervising Set Builder

109. Supervisor

110. Foreman

111. Lead Person

112. Carpenter

113. Assistant Carpenter

114. Key Painter

115. Painter

Hoan (tsuzuku):
Hoh-ahn (tsoo-zoo-koo):

103. Heitai
     Hay-tye

104. Suihei
     Soo-ee-hay

105. Kaiheitai-in
     Kye-hay-tye-een

106. Engan Keibitai-in
     Ehn-gahn Kay-bee-tye-een

107. Soobooshi
     Soh'oh-boh'oh-shee

Oodoogu:
Oh'oh-doh'oh-goo:

108. Oodoogu Shunin
     Oh'oh-doh'oh-goo Shoo-neen

109. Kanrisha/Suupaabaizaa
     Kahn-ree-shah/Soo'oo-pah'ah-bye-zah-ah

110. Shunin
     Shoo-neen

111. Riidaa
     Ree'ee-dah'ah

112. Daiku
     Dye-koo

113. Daiku Joshu
     Dye-koo Joh-shoo

114. Tosoo Shunin
     Toh-soh'oh Shoo-neen

115. Tosoo Gakari
     Toh-soh'oh Gah-kah-ree

Set Construction (continued):

116. Sign Writer

117. Draper

118. Upholsterer

119. Paperhanger

120. Tiler

121. Plasterer

122. Plumber

123. Electrician

124. Model Builder

125. Prop Maker

Sound:

126. Mixer

127. Recordist

128. Boom Person

Oodoogu (tsuzuku):
Oh'oh-doh'oh-goo (tsoo-zoo-koo):

116. Sainkaki
     Syne-kah-kee

117. Kaatenhari
     Kah'ah-tehn-hah-ree

118. Kaguseizoo
     Kah-goo-say-zoh'oh

119. Kabegami
     Kah-beh-gah-mee

120. Tairuhari
     Tye-roo-hah-ree

121. Sakan
     Sah-kahn

122. Haikankoo
     Hye-kahn-koh'oh

123. Denkikoo
     Dehn-kee-koh'oh

124. Mokeiseizoo
     Moh-kay-say-koh'oh

125. Kodoogu Shunin
     Koh-doh'oh-goo Shoo-neen

Onsei:
Ohn-say:

126. Mikisaa
     Mee-kee-sah'ah

127. Rokuon Gishi
     Roh-koo-ohn Gee-shee

128. Buumu Soosain
     Boo'oom Soh'oh-syne

Sound (continued):

129. Cable Person

130. Newsreel

131. Playback Operator

132. Re-recording Mixer

133. Music/Sound Effects Mixer

134. Maintenance Engineer

Transportation:

135. Driver Foreman

136. Chauffeur

137. Truck Driver

138. Camera Car

139. Stunt Car

140. Dispatcher

141. Mechanic

Onsei (tsuzuku):
Ohn-say (tsoo-zoo-koo):

129. Keeburu Soosain
     Keh'eh-boo-roo Soh'oh-syne

130. Nyuusu Eiga
     N'yoo'oos Ay-gah

131. Saisei Soosain
     Sye-say Soh'oh-syne

132. Sai-rokuon Mikisaa
     Sye-roh-koo-ohn Mee-kee-sah'ah

133. Onkyoo Kooka Mikisaa
     Ohn-k'yoh'oh Koh'oh-kah Mee-kee-sah'ah

134. Hoshu Gijitsusha
     Hoh-shoo Gee-jee-tsoo-shah

Nakama:
Nah-kah-mah:

135. Unten Shunin
     Oon-tehn Shoo-neen

136. Untenshu
     Oon-tehn-shoo

137. Torakku Untenshu
     Toh-rahk-koo Oon-tehn-shoo

138. Kamera-kaa
     Kah-meh-rah-kah'ah

139. Sutantokaa
     S'tahn-toh-kah'ah

140. Unkoo Kanrisha
     Oon-koh'oh Kahn-ree-shah

141. Shuurikoo
     Shoo'oo-ree-koh'oh

<u>Video</u>:

142. Technical Director

143. Lighting Director

144. Shader

145. Cameraperson

146. Tape Recordist

147. Kine Recordist

148. Telecine Operator

149. Audio Mixer

150. Public Address Operator

151. Floor Manager

152. Video Tape Operator

153. Engineer

154. Maintenance Engineer

155. Technical Coordinator

Bideo:
Bee-deh-oh:

142. Gijutsu Shunin
    Gee-joo-tsoo Shoo-neen

143. Shoomei Shunin
    Shoh'oh-may Shoo-neen

144. Choosei-in
    Choh'oh-say-een

145. Kameraman
    Kah-meh-rah-mahn

146. Teepu Rokuongishi
    Teh'eh-poo Roh-koo-ohn-gee-shee

147. Fuirumu Rokugagishi
    Foo-ee-roo-moo Roh-koo-gah-gee-shee

148. Tereshine Soosain
    Teh-reh-shee-neh Soh'oh-syne

149. Oodio Mikisaa
    Oh'oh-dee-oh Mee-kee-sah'ah

150. Kakusei Soochi Soosain
    Kah-k'say Soh'oh-chee Soh'oh-syne

151. Furoaa Maneejaa
    Foo-roh-ah'ah Mah-neh'eh-jah'ah

152. Bideo Teepu Soosain
    Bee-deh-oh Teh'eh-poo Soh'oh-syne

153. Gijutsu-sha
    Gee-joo-tsoo-shah

154. Hoshu Gijutsu-sha
    Hoh-shoo Gee-joo-tsoo-shah

155. Gijutsu Choosei-in
    Gee-joo-tsoo Choh'oh-say-een

Video (continued):

156. Associate Director

157. Cue Card Person

158. Cable Person

159. Switcher (Vision Mixer)

WARDROBE:

160. Key Wardrobe

161. Assistant Wardrobe

162. Costumer

163. Dresser

164. Fitter

165. Tailor

Bideo (tsuzuku):
Bee-deh-oh (tsoo-zoo-koo):

156. Jokantoku
     Joh-kahn-toh-koo

157. Kyuu-kaado Yooin
     K'yoo'oo-kah'ah-doh Yoh-oyn

158. Keeburu Soosain
     Keh'eh-boo-roo Soh'oh-syne

159. Suicchaa
     Soo-eet-chah'ah

Ishoo Bu:
Ee-shoh'oh Boo:

160. Ishoo Shunin
     Ee-shoh'oh Shoo-neen

161. Ishoo Joshu
     Ee-shoh'oh Joh-shoo

162. Kosuchuumaa
     Koh-soo-choo'oo-mah'ah

163. Kitsuke Gakari/Doressaa
     Kee-ts'keh Gah-kah-ree/Doh-rehs-sah'ah

164. Karinui Gakari/Fittaa
     Kah-ree-noo-ee Gah-kah-ree/Fee-tah'ah

165. Shitate Gakari
     Shee-tah-teh Gah-kah-ree

01. Ready

02. Silence

03. Roll camera

04. Roll tape

05. Speed!

06. Slate

07. Mark it!

08. One moment

09. Action!

10. Cut

11. Print it

12. How was that?

13. Good take

14. No good

15. Fair

STEEJI YOOGO   15
STEH'EH-JEE YOH'OH-GOH

01. Yooi
    Yoh-oy

02. Shizukani
    Shee-zoo-kah-nee

03. Kamera o mawase
    Kah-meh-rah oh mah-wah-seh

04. Teepu o mawase
    Teh'eh-poo oh mah-wah-seh

05. Supeedo o awasete
    Soo-peh'eh-doh oh áh-wah-seh-teh

06. Kachinko
    Kah-cheen-koh

07. Maaku shite
    Mah'ah-koo shee-teh

08. Chotto matte
    Choht-toh maht-teh

09. Akushon
    Ah-koo-shohn

10. Katto
    Kaht-toh

11. Purinto shite
    P'reen-toh shee-teh

12. Doo-datta?
    Doh'oh-daht-tah

13. Yoi/Yoshi/"OK"-da
    Yoy/Yoh-shee/Oh-Kay-dah

14. Dame
    Dah-meh

15. I-ideshoo
    Ee-ee-deh-shoh'oh

16. Excellent

17. Missed the mark

18. Missed the cue

19. Too early

20. Too late

21. Once more

22. Clear (the view of) camera

23. What is next?

24. Another angle

25. Another set-up

26. Our next shot is -- .

27. A _____ shot:

  a.   dolly

  b.   crane

  c.   lockdown

16. Subarashi-i
    Soo-bah-rah-shee-ee

17. Maaku o minogashita
    Mah'ahk oh mee-noh-gah-shee-tah

18. Kyuu o minogashita
    K'yoo'oo oh mee-noh-gah-shee-tah

19. Hayasugiru
    Hah-yah-soo-gee-roo

20. Ososugiru
    Oh-soh-soo-gee-roo

21. Moo-ichido
    Moh'oh-ee-chee-doh

22. Kamera no mae o akete
    Kah-meh-rah noh mah-eh oh ah-keh-teh

23. Tsugi wa nandesuka?
    Tsoo-gee wah nahn-dehs-kah?

24. Betsu no anguru kara
    Beh-tsoo noh ahn-goo-roo kah-rah

25. Betsu no setto
    Beh-tsoo noh seht-toh

26. Tsugi no shotto wa ___ desu
    Tsoo-gee noh shoht-toh wah ___ dehs

27. ___ shotto:
    sshoht-toh:

 a. Daisha/Doorii-
    Dye-shah/Doh'oh-ree'ee-

 b. Kureen-
    Koo-reh'ehn-

 c. Kotei-
    Koh-tay-

28. Lay down dolly:

  a.   boards

  b.   track

29. Start here

30. End there

31. Start there

32. End here

33. How long will it take?

34. How much time do we have?

35. When will this be ready?

36. I do not know

37. Who knows?

38. There will be a short delay

39. Why the delay?

40. There is a need for...

28. Daisha o oroshite:
    Dye-shah oh oh-roh-shee-teh:

  a.   Itajiki-
       Ee-tah-jee-kee-

  b.   Reeru tsuki-
       Reh'eh-roo tsoo-kee-

29. Kokode hajimete
    Koh-koh-deh hah-jee-meh-teh

30. Sokode owatte
    Soh-koh-deh oh-wah-teh

31. Sokode hajimete
    Soh-koh-deh hah-jee-meh-teh

32. Kokode owatte
    Koh-koh-deh oh-wah-teh

33. Doregurai kakarimasuka?
    Doh-reh-goo-rye kah-kah-ree-mahs-kah?

34. Doregurai jikan ga arimasuka?
    Doh-reh-goo-rye jee-kahn gah ah-ree-mahs-ka?

35. Itsu yooi ga dekimasuka?
    Ee-tsoo yoh-oy gah deh-kee-mahs-ka?

36. Shirimasen
    Shee-ree-mah-sehn

37. Dare ga shitte imasuka?
    Dah-reh gah sh't-teh ee-mahs-kah?

38. Chotto okuremasu
    Choht-toh oh-koo-reh-mahs

39. Dooshite okureru no desuka?
    Doh'oh-sh'teh oh-koo-reh-roo noh des-kah?

40. ___ ga hitsuyoodesu
    ___ gah hee-tsoo-yoh'oh-dehs

41. Adjusting a light

42. Waiting for the sun

43. Light them up! (luminaires)

44. Shake them up! (reflectors)

45. Ready for the actors

46. On stage

47. On location

48. Anytime you are ready

49. With your permission

50. Check makeup

51. Check hair

52. Check costume

53. Too much

54. Not enough

55. More

41. Raito no choosei
    Rye-toh noh cho'oh-say

42. Taiyoo-machi
    Tye-yoh'oh-mah-chee

43. Motto akaruku!
    Moht-toh ah-kah-roo-koo!

44. Yoko fure!
    Yoh-koh foo-reh!

45. Shutsuensha junbi yoroshi-i
    Shoo-tsoo-ehn-shah joon-bee yoh-roh-shee-
                                          ee
46. Suteeji de
    Soo-teh'eh-jee deh

47. Rokeishon de
    Roh-kay-shohn deh

48. Junbi dekishidai itsudemo
    Joon-bee deh-kee-shee-dye ee-tsoo-deh-moh

49. Anata no kyoka o ete
    Ah-nah-tah noh k'yoh-kah oh eh-teh

50. Meikuappu o shirabete
    May-kahp oh shee-rah-beh-teh

51. Heaa o shirabete
    Heh-ah'ah o shee-rah-beh-teh

52. Kosuchuumu o shirabete
    Koh-soo-choo'oo-moo oh shee-rah-beh-teh

53. Oosugiru
    Oh'oh-soo-gee-roo

54. Fujuubun
    Foo-joo'oo-boon

55. Motto
    Moht-toh

56. Less

57. Yes

58. No

59. Perhaps

60. Who

61. What

62. Where

63. Why

64. When

65. Tall

66. Long

67. Short

68. Squat

69. Help

70. Push

56. Sukunai
   Soo-koo-nye

57. Hai
   Hye

58. Iie
   Ee'ee-eh

59. Tabun
   Tah-boon

60. Dare
   Dah-reh

61. Nani
   Nah-nee

62. Dokode
   Doh-koh-deh

63. Naze
   Nah-zeh

64. Itsu
   Ee-tsoo

65. Takai
   Tah-kye

66. Nagai
   Nah-gye

67. Mijikai
   Mee-jee-kye

68. Shagamu
   Shah-gah-moo

69. Tasukeru
   Tahs-keh-roo

70. Osu
   Oh-soo

71. Pull

72. Wait

73. Now

74. Slower

75. Faster

76. Attention everyone!

77. Wrong set

78. Wrong location

79. It's a move

80. Breakfast

81. Lunch

82. Dinner

83. Take a break

84. Where is the bathroom?

85. We are finished for today

71. Hiku
    Hee-koo

72. Matsu
    Mah-tsoo

73. Ima
    Ee-mah

74. Motto yukkuri
    Moht-toh yook-koo-ree

75. Motto hayaku
    Moht-toh hah-yah-koo

76. Zen-in chuui
    Zehn-een choo'oo-ee

77. Setto ga chigau
    Seht-toh gah chee-g'ow

78. Basho ga chigau
    Bah-shoh gah chee-g'ow

79. Idoo shiyoo
    Ee-doh'oh shee-yoh'oh

80. Chooshoku
    Choh'oh-shoh-koo

81. Chuushoku
    Choo'oo-shoh-koo

82. Yuushoku
    Yoo'oo-shoh-koo

83. Kyuukei
    K'yoo'oo-kay

84. Toire/Gofujoo wa doko desuka?
    Toy-reh/Goh-foo-joh'oh wa doh-koh des-kah?

85. Kyoo wa korede owarimasu
    K'yoh'oh wa koh-reh-deh oh-wah-ree-mahs

86. Crew call for tomorrow is...

87. Same time tomorrow

88. Different time tomorrow

89. Check the schedule

90. Weather permitting

91. When we start again...

92. I would like to see...

93. Would it be possible?

94. Anything you want

95. How soon?

96. All it takes is time and money

97. The most important words

    on any set are:

 a. Please

 b. Thank you

86. Asu no kuruu wa ___ desu
    Ah-soo noh koo-roo'oo wah ___ dehs

87. Asu onaji jikoku
    Ah-soo oh-nah-jee jee-koh-koo

88. Asu betsu no jikoku
    Ah-soo beh-tsoo noh jee-koh-koo

89. Sukejuuru o shirabete
    S'keh-joo'oo-roo oh shee-rah-beh-teh

90. Tenki ga yokereba
    Tehn-kee gah yoh-keh-reh-bah

91. Tsugi ni ___ suruno wa itsu desuka?
    Tsoo-gee nee ___ s'roo-noh wah ee-tsoo des-kah

92. ___ ni aitai
    ___ nee eye-tye

93. ___ dekimasuka?
    ___ deh-kee-mahs-kah?

94. Hoshi-i-mono wa nandemo
    Hoh-shee-ee-moh-noh wah nahn-deh-moh

95. Itsu?
    Ee-tsoo?

96. Jikan to kane dakega kakaru
    Jee-kahn toh kah-neh dah-keh-gah kah-kah-roo

97. Chuui: Dono setto demo ichiban
    Choo'oo-ee: Doh-noh seht-toh deh-moh ee-chee-bahn

           juuyoona kotoba:
           joo-oo-yoh'oh-nah koh-toh-bah:

a. "Doozo"
    "Doh'oh-zoh"

b. "Arigatoo"
    "Ah-ree-gah-toh'oh"

01. Aperture

02. Aperture Plate

03. Barney

04. Battery

05. Black Bag

06. Blimp

07. Body Brace

08. Buckle-trip

09. Cable

10. Camera:

a. base

b. grease

c. oil

d. report

e. tape

Kah-meh-rah

01. Kaikoobu
    Kye-koh'oh-boo

02. Apaachaa Ban
    Ah-pah'ah-chah'ah Bahn

03. Kamerayoo Ooi
    Kah-meh-rah-yoh'oh Oh-oy

04. Denchi
    Dehn-chee

05. Anbako
    Ahn-bah-koh

06. Kamerayoo Ooi
    Kah-meh-rah-yoh'oh Oh-oy

07. Kamera Sasae
    Kah-meh-rah Sah-sah-eh

08. Fuirumu Tsumari Kenshutsu Soochi
    Foo-ee-roo-moo Tsoo-mah-ree Kehn-shoo-tsoo Soh'oh-chee

09. Keeburu/Densen
    Keh'eh-boo-roo/Dehn-sehn

10. Kamera:
    Kah-meh-rah:

  a.   -dai
       -dye

  b.   -guriisu
       -goo-ree'ees

  c.   -abura
       -ah-boo-rah

  d.   -hookoku
       -hoh'oh-koh-koo

  e.   -teepu
       -teh'eh-poo

11. Changing Bag.

12. Close-up

13. Composition

14. Counter:

  a.   digital

  b.   light emitting diode (LED)

15. Darkroom

16. Darkroom Load

17. Day Filming

18. Day-For-Night

19. Daylight Load

20. Depth Of Field

21. Depth Of Focus

22. Diopter (lens)

23. Ditty Bag

11. Fuirumu Kookanyoo Fukuro
    Foo-ee-roo-moo Koh'oh-kahn-yoh'oh Foo-koo-
    *   roh*

12. Kinsetsu Satsuei/Kuroozu Appu
    Keen-seh-tsoo Saht-soo-ay/Koo-roh'oh-zoo
    *   Ahp-poo*

13. Kumiawase/Koosei
    Koo-mee-ah-wah-seh/Koh'oh-say

14. Kauuntaa:
    K'ow'n-tah'ah:

    a.   Dejitaru-
         Deh-jee-tah-roo-

    b.   Hakkoo Daioodo-
         Hahk-koh'oh Dye-oh'oh-doh-

15. Anshitsu
    Ahn-shee-tsoo

16. Anshitsu Sooten
    Ahn-shee-tsoo   Soh'oh-tehn

17. Nicchuu
    Neet-choo'oo

18. Hiruma Satsuei no Yakan Shiin
    Hee-roo-mah Saht-soo-ay noh Yah-kahn
    *   Shee'een*

19. Meishitsu Sooten
    May-shee-tsoo Soh'oh-tehn

20. Hishakai Shindo
    Hee-shah-kye Sheen-doh

21. Shooten Shindo
    Shoh'oh-tehn Sheen-doh

22. Shido/Jioputoru
    Shee-doh/Jee-oh-poo-toh-roo

23. Komonoire
    Koh-moh-noy-reh

24. Dolly Shot

25. Eyepiece

26. Exterior

27. Fast

28. Film jam

29. Filter:

  a.   conversion

  b.   graduated

  c.   neutral density

  d.   polarizing

  e.   sky

  f.   star

  g.   fog

  h.   fluorescent

30. Filter Holder

24. Daisha Joo Shotto
    Dye-shah Joh'oh Shoht-toh

25. Setsuganbu/Ai-piisu
    Seh-tsoo-gahn-boo/Eye-pee'ees

26. Gaibu
    Gye-boo

27. Hayai
    Hah-y'eye

28. Fuirumu no Tsumari
    Foo-ee-roo-moo no Tsoo-mah-ree

29. Fuirutaa:
    Foo-ee-roo-tah'ah:

a. Henkan-
   Hehn-kahn-

b. Dankai-
   Dahn-kye-

c. Enu-jii-
   Ehn-jee'ee-

d. Henkoo-
   Hehn-koo-

e. Sukairaito-
   Soo-k'eye-rye-toh-

f. Sutaa-
   S'tah'ah-

g. Bokashi-
   Boh-kah-shee-

h. Keikoo-
   Kay-koo-

30. Fuirutaa Horudaa
    Foo-ee-roo-tah'ah Hoh-roo-dah'ah

31. Flare

32. Focus:

a. follow-

b. -knob

c. mark

d. out-of-

e. sharp

33. Follow Shot

34. Frame

35. Frameline

36. Frames Per Second (fps)

37. Gate

38. Gear

39. Hair-check

40. High Angle

31. Fureaa
    Foo-reh-ah'ah

32. Shooten:
    Shoh'oh-ten:

   a. -forou
       -foh-roh

   b. -tsumami
       -tsoo-mah-mee

   c. -maaku
       -mah'ah-koo

   d. -zure
       -zoo-reh

   e. Senmeina-
       Sehn-may-nah-

33. Nagashidori
    Nah-gah-shee-doh-ree

34. Waku
    Wah-koo

35. Waku o Shimesu Sen
    Wah-koo oh Shee-meh-soo Sehn

36. Koma/Byoo
    Koh-mah/B'yoh'oh

37. Kaikoobu/Geeto
    Kye-koh'oh-boo/Geh-eh-toh

38. Haguruma
    Hah-goo-roo-mah

39. Apaachaa no Chekku
    Ah-pah'ah-chah'ah noh Chek-koo

40. Takai Kakudo
    Tah-kye Kah-koo-doh

41. Hold

42. Insert

43. Interior

44. Intermittant

45. Lens

46. Lens Cleaner

47. Lens Mount

48. Level

49. Lockdown Screw

50. Long Shot

51. Low Angle

52. Magazine:

  a. co-axial

  b. displacement

  c. feed side

41. Hoji
    Hoh-jee

42. Soonyuu
    Soh'oh-n'yoo'oo

43. Naibu
    Nye-boo

44. Kanketsuteki
    Kahn-keh-tsoo-teh-kee

45. Renzu
    Rehn-zoo

46. Renzu Seisoo Yoogo
    Rehn-zoo Say-soh'oh Yoh'oh-goh

47. Renzu Maunto
    Rehn-zoo M'ow'n-toh

48. Suihei
    Soo-ee-hay

49. Kotei Neji
    Koh-tay Neh-jee

50. Hiroi Shotto
    Hee-roy Shoht-toh

51. Hikui Kakudo
    Hee-koo-ee Kah-kah-doh

52. Magajin:
    Mah-gah-jeen:

  a. Doojiki-
    Doh'oh-jee-kee-

  b. Torihazushi-
    Toh-ree-hah-zoo-shee-

  c. Kuridashi Gawa-
    Koo-ree-dah-shee Gah-wah-

52. Magazine (continued):

  d. lid

  e. lighttrap

  f. spindle wheel

  g. take-up side

  h. throat

53. Masking Tape

54. Matte

55. Matte-box

56. Medium Shot

57. Meter:

  a. incident

  b. reflectance

  c. spot

  d. color temperature

52. Magajin (tsuzuku):
    Mah-gah-jeen (tsoo-zoo-koo):

  d.   -futa
         -foo-tah

  e.   -shakoo
         -shah-koh'oh

  f.   -supindoru guruma
         s'pin-doh-roo goo-roo-mah

  g.   Makitori gawa-
         Mah-kee-toh-ree gah-wah

  h.   -fuirumu deguchi
         -foo-ee-roo-moo deh-goo-chee

53. Masuku Teepu
    Mah-soo-koo Teh'eh-poo

54. Matto Men
    Maht-toh Mehn

55. Renzu Ooi Bako
    Rehn-zoo Oh-oy Bah-koh

56. Chuukan no Shottoh
    Choo'oo-kahn noh Shoh-toh

57. Roshutsu
    Roh-shoo-tsoo

  a.   chokusetsu gata
         choh-koo-seh-tsoo gah-tah

  b.   hansha shiki
         hahn-shah shee-kee

  c.   supotto shiki
         s'poht-toh shee-kee

  d.   iro ondo
         ee-roh ohn-doh

58. Motion Picture Camera

59. Motor:

  a.   animation

  b.   crystal-controlled

  c.   time-lapse

  d.   intermittant

  e.   slow-motion

  f.   high-speed

  g.   very-high-speed

  h.   ultra-high-speed

60. Movement:

  a.   pulldown claw

  b.   registration-pin

61. Night Filming

62. On/Off Switch

58. Eiga Yoo Kamera
    Ay-gah Yoh'oh Kah-meh-rah

59. Mootaa:
    Moh'oh-tah'ah:

 a.   animeeshon
      ah-nee-meh'eh-shohn

 b.   kurisutaru kontorooru
      koo-rees'tah-roo kohn-toh-roh'oh-roo

 c.   jikan keika
      jee-kahn kay-kah

 d.   kanketsuteki
      kahn-keh-tsoo-teh-kee

 e.   suroo mooshon
      soo-roh'oh moh'oh-shohn

 f.   Koosokudo/Hai supiido
      koh'oh-soh-koo-doh/hye s'pee'ee-doh

 g.   choo koosokudo
      choh'oh koh'oh-soh-koo-doh

 h.   goku choo koosokudo
      goh-koo choh'oh koh'oh-soh-koo-doh

60. Doosa:
    Doh'oh-sah:

 a.   kakiotoshi zume
      kah-kee-oh-toh-shee zoo-meh

 b.   ichigime pin
      ee-chee-gee-meh peen

61. Yakan Satsuei
    Yah-kahn Sah-tsoo-ay

62. Suicchi
    Soo-eet-chee

63. Over-the-shoulder

64. Pan:

   a.   left

   b.   right

65. Pan Handle

66. Pan Lock

67. Parallax

68. Periscope Finder

69. Pressure-pad

70. Printed Take

71. Process Shot:

   a.   blue screen

   b.   front projection

   c.   rear projection

   d.   traveling-matte

63. Katagoshi
    Kah-tah-goh-shee

64. Pan:
    Pahn:

  a.   hidari
       hee-dah-ree

  b.   migi
       mee-gee

65. Pan Boo
    Pahn Boh'oh

66. Pan Kotei
    Pahn Koh-tay

67. Shisa
    Shee-sah

68. Perisukoopu Faindaa
    Peh-ree-s'koh'oh-poo Fye'n-dah'ah

69. Acchaku Paddo
    Ahk-chah-koo Pahd-doh

70. Saiyoo Purinto
    Sye-yoh'oh Poo-reen-toh

71. Goosei Shotto:
    Goh'oh-say Shoht-toh:

  a.   buruu sukuriin
       b'roo'oo s'koo-ree'een

  b.   zenpoo soonyuu
       zehn-poh'oh soh'oh-n'yoo'oo

  c.   koohoo soonyuu
       koh'oh-hoh'oh soh'oh-n'yoo'oo

  d.   idooshiki kakiwari
       ee-doh'oh-shee-kee kah-kee-wah-ree

72. Rackover

73. Receptacle

74. Re-load

75. Re-take

76. Reverse Angle

77. Roller

78. Safe-action-area

79. Shipping label

80. Shoulder-pod

81. Shutter:

a. fixed

b. variable

c. mirror-reflex

d. butterfly

e. open-segment

72. Taretto Shiki Renzu Kookan
    Tah-reht-toh Shee-kee Rehn-zoo Koo-kahn

73. Riseputakuru
    Ree-sehp'tah-koo-roo

74. Sai Sooten
    Sye Soh'oh-tehn

75. Sai Satsuei
    Sye Sah-tsoo-ay

76. Gyaku Anguru
    G'yah-koo Ahn-goo-roo

77. Rooraa
    Roh'oh-rah'ah

78. Anzen Chitai
    Ahn-zehn Chee-tye

79. Okurisaki Raberu
    Oh-koo-ree-sah-kee Rah-beh-roo

80. Kata Poddo
    Kah-tah Pohd-doh

81. Shattaa:
    Shaht-tah'ah:

   a.   kotei
         koh-tay

   b.   kahen
         kah-hen

   c.   miraa hansha shiki
         mee-rah'ah hahn-shah shee-kee

   d.   choo gata
         choh'oh gah-tah

   e.   kaikoobu
         kye-koh'oh-boo

82. Sequence

83. Slate

84. Spreader

85. Speed:

   a. fast

   b. slow

   c. high

   d. synchronous

   e. variable

86. Sprocket

87. Still Camera

88. Stop (lens)

89. Stop (camera)

90. Tachometer

91. Take

82. Renzoku
    Rehn-zoh-koo

83. Kachinko
    Kah-cheen-koh

84. Sankyaku
    Sahn-k'yahk

85. Sokudo:
    Soh-koo-doh:

  a.   hayai
        hah-y'eye

  b.   osoi
        oh-soy

  c.   koo
        koh'oh

  d.   doochoo/sinku
        doh'oh-choh'oh/seen-koo

  e.   kahen shiki
        kah-hen shee-kee

86. Supuroketto
    S'p'roh-keht-toh

87. Suchiiru Kamera
    S'chee'ee-roo Kah-meh-rah

88. Akarusa
    Ah-kah-roo-sah

89. Tomete/Stoppu
    Toh-meh-teh/Stohp-poo

90. Kaiten Kei/Tako Meetaa
    Kye-tehn Kay/Tah-koh Meh'eh-ta'ah

91. Saiyoo
    Sye-yoh'oh

92. Take-up

93. Take-up Belt

94. Telephoto

95. Test

96. Threading

97. Three-shot

98. Tie-down Chain

99. Tilt:

  a.   down

  b.   up

100. Tilt Plate

101. Timing Gear

102. Turret

103. Tripod:

  a.   standard legs

92. Makitori
    Mah-kee-toh-ree

93. Makitori Beruto
    Mah-kee-toh-ree Beh-roo-toh

94. Booen
    Boh'oh-ehn

95. Shiken
    Shee-kehn

96. Fuirumu
    Foo-ee-roo-moo

97. San-nin o Utsusu Shotto
    Sahn-neen oh Oo-tsoo-soo Shoht-toh

98. Kotei Chieen
    Koh-tay Chee-eh'ehn

99. Joogedo/Chiruto:
    Joh'oh-geh-doh/Chee-roo-toh:

   a. shita
       shee-tah

   b. ue
       oo-eh

100. Chiruto Ban
     Chee-roo-toh Bahn

101. Taimingu Haguruma
     Tye-meen-goo Hah-goo-roo-mah

102. Taaretto
     Tah'ah-reht-toh

103. Sankyaku:
     Sahn-k'yah-koo:

   a. tsuujoogata no ashi
       tsoo'oo-joh'oh-gah-tah no ah-shee

103. Tripod (cont):

  b.   medium legs

  c.   baby legs

  d.   hi-hat

104. Tripod Handle

105. Tripod Head:

  a.   slip

  b.   fluid

  c.   geared

106. Tripod Parts:

  a.   legs

  b.   shoe

  c.   point

  d.   spur

  e.   adjusting knobs

103. Sankyaku (tsuzuku):
     Sahn-k'yah-koo (tsoo-zoo-koo)

   b.   chuukan nagas no ashi
             choo'oo-kahn nah-gahs noh ah-shee

   c.   kogata no ashi
             koh-gah-tah noh ah-shee

   d.   koteishiki kogata sankyaku
             koh-tay-shee-kee koh-gah-tah sahn-
                                               k'yah-koo

104. Sankyaku Handoru
     Sahn-k'yah-koo Hahn-doh-roo

105. Undai:
     Oon-dye:

   a.   surippu shiki
             soo-reep-poo shee-kee

   b.   ryuutai shiki
             r'yoo'oo-tye shee-kee

   c.   gia shiki
             gee-ah shee-kee

106. Sankyaku Yoo Buhin:
     Sahn-k'yah-koo Yoh'oh Boo-heen

   a.   ashi
             ah-shee

   b.   shuu
             shoo'oo

   c.   pointo
             poyn-toh

   d.   supaa
             s'pah'ah

   e.   choosei nobu
             choh'oh-say noh-boo

107. Two-shot

108. Viewfinder:

   a. reflex

   b. offset

109. Wide-angle

110. Zoom Shot

Useful Terms:

111. Exposed Film

112. Raw Stock

113. Short End

114. Ship Air Express

115. Special Handling

116. Airbill Number

117. Waybill number

118. Packing Slip Enclosed

107. Futari Ireru Shotto
     Foo-tah-ree Ee-reh-roo Shoht-toh

108. Faindaa:
     Fye'n-dah'ah:

   a. hansha
       hahn-shah

   b. ofusetto
       ohf-seht-toh

109. Kookaku
     Koh'oh-kah-koo

110. Zuumu Shotto
     Zoo'oo-moo Shoht-toh

Yakunitatsu Kotoba:
Yahk-nee-tah-tsoo Koh-toh-bah:

111. Satsueizumi Fuirumu
     Sah-tsoo-ay-zoo-mee Foo-ee-roo-moo

112. Misatsuei Fuirumu
     Mee-sah-tsoo-ay Foo-ee-roo-moo

113. Ichibu Setsudanzumi Fuirumu
     Ee-chee-boo Seh-tsoo-dahn-zoo-mee Foo-
     ee-roo-moo

114. Kooku Shikyuubin
     Koh'oh-koo Shee-k'yoo'oo-been

115. Tokushu Toriatsukai
     Toh-koo-shoo Toh-ree-ah-tsoo-kye

116. Kookuu Unsoo Shorui Bangoo
     Koh'oh-koo'oo Oon-soh'oh Shoh-roo-ee
     Bahn-goh'oh

117. Unsoo Shorui Bangoo
     Oon-soh'oh Shoh-roo-ee Bahn-goh'oh

118. Meisaisho Doofuu
     May-sye-shoh Doh'oh-foo'oo

01. Advanced Sync

02. Background

03. Bench

04. Bin

05. Black-and-White (B&W):

a.   film

b.   negative

c.   original

d.   print

e.   reversal

06. Blow-up

07. Cement

08. Cleaner

09. Coding

01. Zenpoo ni Aru Doochoo Ichi
    Zehn-poh'oh nee Ah-roo Doh'oh-choh'oh Ee-
    chee

02. Haikei
    Hye-kay

03. Benchi
    Behn-chee

04. Tana
    Tah-nah

05. Shiro Kuro:
    Shee-roh Koo-roh:

  a.   -fuirumu
    -foo-ee-roo-moo

  b.   -nega/-inga
    -neh-gah/-een-gah

  c.   -orijinaru
    -oh-ree-jee-nah-roo

  d.   -purinto
    -poo-reen-toh

  e.   -ribaasaru
    -ree-bah'ah-sah-roo

06. Hikinobashi
    Hee-kee-noh-bah-shee

07. Secchakuzai
    Seht-chah-koo-zye

08. Seisoo Yoogu
    Say-soh'oh Yoh'oh-goh

09. Koodingu
    Koh'oh-deen-goo

10. Color:

a. film

b. negative

c. original

d. print

e. reversal

11. Composite Daily

12. Counter:

a. footage

b. metric

c. digital

d. light emitting diode (LED)

13. Credits

14. Cut

15. Cutter

10. Iro/Karaa:
    Ee-roh/Kah-rah'ah:

  a. -fuirumu
     -foo-ee-roo-moo

  b. -nega
     -neh-gah

  c. -orijinaru
     -oh-ree-jee-nah-roo

  d. -purinto
     -poo-reen-toh

  e. -ribaasaru
     -ree-bah'ah-sah-rooh

11. Onsei Henshuu Sareteinai Fuirumu
    Ohn-say Heh-shoo Sah-reh-tay-nye Foo-ee-roo-moo

12. Kauntaa:
    K'ow'n-tah'ah:

  a. fiito suu
     fee'ee-toh soo'oo

  b. meetoru
     meh'eh-toh-roo

  c. dejitaru
     deh-jee-tah-roo

  d. hakko daioodo
     hahk-koh dye-oh'oh-doh

13. Jimaku
    Jee-mah-koo

14. Katto
    Kaht-toh

15. Kattaa
    Kaht-tah'ah

16. Dailies

17. Dead Sync

18. Edge-number

19. Editing Machine:

 a. flat bed

 b. upright

20. Editorial Process

21. Editorial Sync

22. Fade-in

23. Fade-out

24. Fine Cut

25. Fine Grain

26. Frame

27. Frameline

28. Frameline Dirt

16. Sokujitsu Genzoo
    Soh-koo-jeet-soo Gehn-zoh'oh

17. Kanzen-na Doochoo
    Kahn-zen-nah Doh'oh-choh'oh

18. Ejji Nanbaa
    Ehj-jee Nahn-bah'ah

19. Henshuuki:
    Hen-shoo'oo-kee:

   a. hiragata beddo
      hee-rah-gah-tah behd-doh

   b. tategata beddo
      tah-teh-gah-tah behd-doh

20. Henshuu Purosesu
    Hen-shoo Poo-roh-seh-soo

21. Henshuu Dankai no Doochoo Ichi
    Hen-shoo Dahn-kye noh Doh'oh-choh'oh Ee-chee

22. Feido In
    Fay-doh Een

23. Feido Auto
    Fay-doh Ow-toh

24. Saishuu Henshuu Fuirumu
    Sye-shoo'oo Hen-shoo Foo-ee-roo-moo

25. Biryuushi
    Bee-r'yoo'oo-shee

26. Waku/Fureemu
    Wah-koo/Foo-reh'eh-moo

27. Fureemu Rain
    Foo-reh'eh-moo Rye'n

28. Fureemu Rain Joono Gomi
    Foo-reh'eh-moo Rye'n Joh'oh-noh Goh-mee

29. Intercut

30. Interlock

31. Laboratory

32. Lab Report

33. Leader:

  a. academy

  b. black

  c. clear

  d. colored

  e. filler

  f. opaque

  g. white

34. Light Box

35. Magnetic

36. Marking Pen

29. Tochuu Setsudan
    Toh-choo'oo Seh-tsoo-dahn

30. Intaa Rokku
    Een-tah'ah Rohk-koo

31. Genzoojyo
    Gehn-zoh'oh-j'yoh

32. Genzoojyo Karano Repooto
    Gehn-zoh'oh-j'yoh Kah-rah-noh Reh-poh'oh-
                                                  toh

33. Riidaa:
    Ree'ee-dah'ah:

  a. suuji iri
    soo'oo-jee ee-ree

  b. kokushoku
    koh-koo-shoh-koo

  c. toomei
    toh'oh-may

  d. iro tsuki
    ee-roh tsoo-kee

  e. poozu settei yoo
    poh'oh-zoo seht-tay yoh'oh

  f. futoomei
    foo-toh'oh-may

  g. hakushoku
    hah-koo-shoh-koo

34. Dengen Bako
    Den-gehn Bah-koh

35. Jiki
    Jee-kee

36. Maaku Pen
    Mah'ah-koo Pehn

37. Negative Scratch

38. Optical Sound

39. Out-takes

40. Picture

41. Positive Scratch

42. Print:

  a.   answer-

  b.   contact-

  c.   one-light-

  d.   optical-

  e.   preview-

  f.   release

  g.   timed-

  h.   trailer

  i.   work-

37. Negajoo no Kizu
Neh-gah-joh'oh noh Kee-zoo

38. Koogaku Shiki Onkyoo
Koh'oh-gah-koo Shee-kee Ohn-k'yoh'oh

39. Fuyoo Fuirumu
Foo-yoh'oh Foo-ee-roo-moo

40. Gazoo
Gah-zoh'oh

41. Pojijoo no Kizo
Poh-jee-joh'oh noh Kee-zoh

42. Purinto:
Poo-reen-toh:

a. saishuu kakunin yoo-
sye-shoo'oo kah-koo-neen yoh'oh-

b. micchaku-
meet-chhah-koo-

c. tanitsukoo-
tah-nee-tsoo-koh'oh-

d. koogaku shiki-
koh'oh-gah-koo shee-kee-

e. yokoku yoo-
yoh-koh-koo yoh'oh-

f. happyoo yoo-
hahp-p'yoh'oh yoh'oh-

g. rokoo hosei zumi-
roh-koh'oh hoh-say zoo-mee-

h. yokoku yoo-
yoh-koh-koo yoh'oh-

i. jooen yoo-
joh'oh-ehn yoh'oh-

43. Printed Takes

44. Print Down

45. Print Up

46. Razor Blade

47. Reader:

  a.   magnetic

  b.   optical

48. Reduction

49. Reel:

  a.   split-

50. Retarded Sync

51. Rewind (noun)

52. Re-wind (verb)

53. Rough Cut

54. Scene

43. Purinto no Saiyoo Bubun
    Poo-reen-toh noh Sye-yoh'oh Boo-boon

44. Kurakusuru Purinto
    Koo-rah-koo-soo-roo Poo-reen-toh

45. Akarukusuru Purinto
    Ah-kah-roo-koo-soo-roo Poo-reen-toh

46. Kamisori no Ha
    Kah-mee-soh-ree noh Hah

47. Riidaa:
    Ree'ee-dah'ah:

   a. jiki shiki
      jee-kee shee-kee

   b. koogaku shiki
      koh'oh-gah-koo shee-kee

48. Shukushoo
    Shoo-koo-shoh'oh

49. Riiru:
    Ree'ee-roo:

   a. bunkai kanoo-
      boon-kye kah-noh'oh-

50. Okureta Doochoo Maaku
    Oh-koo-reh-tah Doh'oh-choh'oh Mah'ah-kee

51. Makimodosu
    Mah-kee-moh-doh-soo

52. Makimodoshi
    Mah-kee-moh-doh-soo

53. Shitami Yoo Zantei Purinto
    Shee-tah-mee Yoh'oh Zahn-tay Poo-reen-toh

54. Shiin
    Shee'een

55. Scissors

56. Scraper

57. Sealing Tape

58. Sequence

59. Shot-size:

 a.   close-up

 b.   extreme close-up

 c.   extreme long shot

 d.   insert

 e.   long shot

 f.   medium shot

 g.   over-the-shoulder

 h.   telephoto

 i.   three-shot

 j.   two-shot

55. Hasami
    Hah-sah-mee

56. Nyuuzai Hakuri Yoogu
    N'yoo'oo-zye Hah-koo-ree Yoh'oh-goo

57. Shiiru Teepu
    Shee'ee-roo Teh'eh-poo

58. Renzoku
    Rehn-zoh-koo

59. Shotto no Ookisa/Shotto saizu:
    Shoht-toh noh Oh'oh-kee-sah/Shoh-to syze:

a. kuroozu appu
   koo-roh'oh-zoo ahp-poo

b. kyokutan na kuroozu appu
   k'yoh-koo-tahn nah koo-roh'oh-zoo ahp-
   poo

c. kyokutan ni hiroi shotto
   k'yoh-koo-tahn nee hee-roy shoht-toh

d. insaato/soonyuu
   een-sah'ah-toh/soh'oh-n'yoo'oo

e. hiroi shotto
   hee-roy shoht-toh

f. chuukan no shotto
   choo'oo-kahn noh shoht-toh

g. kata goshi shotto
   kah-tah goh-shee shoht-toh

h. booen shotto
   boh'oh-ehn shoht-toh

i. san-nin hairu shotto
   sahn-neen hye-roo shoht-toh

j. futari hairu shotto
   foo-tah-ree hye-roo shoht-toh

60. Silent

61. Sound

62. Sound Tape

63. Sound Track:

   a.   composite

   b.   dialogue

   c.   effect

   d.   music

   e.   narration

   f.   optical

64. Splice:

   a.   bevel

   b.   overlap

   c.   straight

   d.   taped

60. Musei
    Moo-say

61. Onsei
    Ohn-say

62. Rokuon Teepu
    Roh-koo-ohn Teh'eh-poo

63. Saundo Torakku:
    S'ow'n-doh Toh-rahk-koo:

 a.   goosei
      goh'oh-say

 b.   kaiwa/daiarogu
      kye-wah/dye-ah-rohg

 c.   kooka
      koh'oh-kah

 d.   ongaku
      ohn-gah-koo

 e.   nareeshon
      nah-reh'eh-shohn

 f.   koogakushiki
      koh'oh-gah-koo-shee-kee

64. Supuraisu:
    Soo-poo-rye-soo:

 a.   naname-
      nah-nah-meh-

 b.   oobaa rappu-
      oh'oh-bah'ah rahp-poo-

 c.   sutoreeto-
      soo-toh-reh'eh-toh-

 d.   teepu de tsunaida-
      teh'eh-poo deh tsoo-nye-dah-

65. Splicer:

a. butt

b. cold

c. hot

66. Splicing Tape:

a. clear

b. color

c. white

67. Synchronizer

68. Sync mark

69. Timing

70. Titles

71. Transfer

72. Trims

73. Viewer

65. Supuraisaa:
    Soo-poo-rye-sah'ah

  a. tsukiawase
      tsoo-kee-ah-wah-seh

  b. teepu shiyoo
      teh'eh-poo shee-yoh'oh

  c. secchakuzai shiyoo
      seht-chah-koo-zye shee-yoh'oh

66. Supuraisingu Teepu:
    Soo-poo-rye-seen-goo Teh'eh-poo:

  a. toomei
      toh'oh-may

  b. karaa
      kah-rah'ah

  c. hakushoku
      hah-koo-shoh-koo

67. Shinkuronaizaa
    Sheen-koo-roh-nye-zah'ah

68. Shinku Maaku
    Sheen-koo Mah'ah-koo

69. Taimingu
    Tye-meen-goo

70. Jimaku
    Jee-mah-koo

71. Tensha
    Tehn-shah

72. Torimu
    Toh-ree-moo

73. Byuaa
    B'yoo-ah'ah

74. Visual Effects:

 a.   cut

 b.   dissolve

 c.   fade-in

 d.   fade-out

 e.   slow cut

 f.   split-screen

 g.   sub-title

 h.   superimpose

 i.   wipe

75. Voice-over

Useful Terms:

76. Do not project!

77. Pick Up From The Laboratory

78. Ready For Sound Mix

74. Shikaku Kooka:
    Shee-kah-koo Koh'oh-kah:

 a.   kyuusoku-na gamen tenkan
       k'yoo'oo-soh-koo-nah gah-men tehn-kahn

 b.   tenkan
       ten-kahn

 c.   feido in
       fay-doh een

 d.   feido auto
       fay-doh ow-toh

 e.   hayai gamen tenkan
       hah-y'eye gah-men tehn-kahn

 f.   bunkatsu sukuriin
       boon-kah-tsoo soo-koo-reen

 g.   jimaku
       jee-mah-koo

 h.   suupaa inpoozu
       soo'oo-pah'ah een-poh'oh-zoo

 i.   gamen no irekawari
       gah-men noh ee-reh-kah-wah-ree

75. Betsu Nareeshon Soonyuu
    Beh-tsoo Nah-reh'eh-shohn Soh'oh-n'yoo'oo

Yakunitatsu Kotoba:
Yahk-nee-tah-tsoo Koh-toh-bah:

76. Tooei Shinaide!
    Toh'oh-ay Shee-nye-dah!

77. Genzoojyo Kara Mottekite
    Gehn-zoo-j'yoh Kah-rah Moht-teh-kee-teh

78. Onsei Mikkusu Dekimasu
    Ohn-say Meek-koo-soo Deh-kee-mahs

Useful Terms (continued):

79. Scene Missing

80. Send To Laboratory

81. To Be Coded

<u>Yakunitatsu Kotoba (tsuzuku)</u>:
Yahk-nee-tah-tsoo Koh-toh-bah (tsoo-zoo-koo):

79. Misatsuei Bubun
    Mee-sah-tsoo-ay Boo-boon

80. Genzoojyoo E Okutte
    Gehn-zoh'oh-j'yoh'oh Eh Oh-koot-teh

81. Koodo O Irerukoto
    Koh'oh-doh Oh Ee-reh-roo-koh-toh

01. Adapter

02. Alternating Current (AC)

03. Aluminum Wire

04. Ambient

05. Ammeter

06. Amperage

07. Ampere

08. Arc Flame

09. Artificial Light

10. Background Light

11. Backlight

12. Bale

13. Ballast

14. Barndoor

01. Adaputaa
    Ah-dah-poo-tah'ah

02. Kooryuu (AC)
    Koh'oh-r'yoh'oh (Ah-Shee'ee)

03. Arumisen
    Ah-roo-mee-sehn

04. Funiki/Anbiento
    Foo-nee-kee/Ahn-bee-ehn-toh

05. Denryuukei
    Dehn-r'yoo'oo-kay

06. Denryuu
    Dehn-r'yoo'oo

07. Anpea
    Ahn-peh-ah

08. Aaku Nonoo
    Ah'ah-koo Noh-noh'oh

09. Jinkoo Raito
    Jeen-koh'oh Rye-toh

10. Haikei Raito
    Hye-kay Rye-toh

11. Koobu Raito
    Koh'oh-boo Rye-toh

12. Beiru
    Bay-roo

13. Barasuto
    Bah-rah-soo-toh

14. Raito ni Tsuiteiru Ita
    Rye-toh nee Tsoo-ee-tay-roo Ee-tah

15. Base:

a.   bayonet

b.   bi-post

c.   mogul

d.   pin

e.   screw

f.   threaded

16. Beam

17. Boomlight

18. Bulb:

a.   clear

b.   frosted

c.   gas-filled

d.   milky

e.   vacuum

15. Dai:
    Dye:

a. bayonetto
   bah-yoh-neht-toh

b. nihon
   nee-hohn

c. mogaru shiki
   moh-gah-roo shee-kee

d. kogata enkei konekutaa
   koh-gah-tah ehn-kay koh-neh-koo-tah'ah

e. neji
   neh-jee

f. nejiyam ga kittearu
   neh-jee-yahm gah keet-teh-ah-roo

16. Biimu
    Bee'ee-moo

17. Buumu Raito
    Boo'oo-moo Rye-toh

18. Denkyuu:
    Den-k'yoo'oo:

a. toomei
   toh'oh-may

b. kumori
   koo-moh-ree

c. gasu iri
   gah-soo ee-ree

d. nyuuhakushoku
   n'yoo'oo-hah-koo-shoh'k

e. shinkuu
   sheen-koo'oo

19. Buss Bar

20. Cable:

a.   single-wire

b.   two-wire

c.   three-wire

d.   ground

e.   negative

f.   neutral

g.   positive

21. Carbon Arc:

a.   feed

b.   gap

c.   crater

d.   flame

e.   grid

19. Boo
    Boh'oh

20. Densen:
    Dehn-sehn:

   a. tanshin
       tahn-sheen

   b. nishin
       nee-sheen

   c. sanshin
       sahn-sheen

   d. aasu
       ah'ah-soo

   e. mainasu
       mye-nah-soo

   f. chuuritsu
       choo'oo-ree-tsoo

   g. purasu
       poo-rah-soo

21. Kaabon Aaku:
    Kah'ah-bohn Ah'ah-koo:

   a. fiido
       fee'ee-doh

   b. sukima
       soo-kee-mah

   c. kureetaa
       koo-reh'eh-tah'ah

   d. hono-o
       hoh-noh-oh

   e. koshi
       koh-shee

21. Carbon Arc (continued):

   f.   striker

   g.   sputter

   h.   hiss

   i.   underflame

   j.   white flame

   k.   yellow flame

22. Carbon Electrode:

   a.   ionized

   b.   positive

   c.   negative

   d.   copper-jacketed

   e.   bullet-nosed

23. Circuit Breaker

24. Cluster Lights

21. Kaabon Aaku (tsuzuku):
    Kah'ah-bohn Ah'ah-koo (tsoo-zoo-koo):

 f. sutoraikaa
    s'toh-rye-kah'ah

 g. pachi pachi on
    pah-chee pah-chee ohn

 h. shuu shuu on
    shoo'oo shoo'oo ohn

 i. denkyoku kara-noh hon-o
    dehn-k'yoh-koo kah-rah-noh hohn-oh

 j. hakushoku hono-o
    hah-koo-shoh-koo hoh-noh-oh

 k. kiiro no hono-o
    kee'ee-roh noh hoh-noh-oh

22. Tanso Denkyoku:
    Tahn-soh Dehn-k'yoh-koo:

 a. ionka sareta
    ee-ohn-kah sah-reh-tah

 b. sei
    say

 c. fu
    foo

 d. doo hifuku
    doh'oh hee-foo-koo

 e. dangan gata
    dahn-gahn gah-tah

23. Shadanki
    Shah-dahn-kee

24. Suugoo Gata Raito
    Soo'oo-goh'oh Gah-tah Rye-toh

25. Color Temperature

26. Color Wheel

27. Compact

28. Connector

29. Copper Wire

30. Counter:

  a.   hourly

  b.   digital

31. Coverage:

  a.   beam

  b.   field

  c.   circular

  d.   elliptical

  e.   rectangular

25. Iro Ondo
    Ee-roh Ohn-doh

26. Kaitenshiki Firutaa Horudaa
    Kye-tehn-shee-kee Fee-roo-tah'ah Hoh-roo-
    dah'ah

27. Kogat
    Koh-gaht

28. Konekutaa
    Koh-neh-koo-tah'ah

29. Doosen
    Doh'oh-sehn

30. Kauntaa:
    K'ow'n-tah'ah:

 a.   keiji
      kay-jee

 b.   dejitaru
      deh-jee-tah-roo

31. Shoomei Han-i:
    Shoh'oh-may Hahn-ee:

 a.   ichijookoo/biimu
      ee-chee-joh'oh-koh'oh/bee'eem

 b.   zentai
      zen-tye

 c.   enkei
      ehn-kay

 d.   daenkei
      dah-ehn-kay

 e.   shikakukei
      shee-kah-koo-kay

32. Connector

a. female-

b. keyed

c. male-

d. pin-

e. stage-

f. straight-blade

g. three-pronged

h. two-pronged

i. twist-lock

33. Current:

a. single-phase

b. three-phase

34. Cut-out Switch

35. Cycle

32. Konekutaa:
    Koh-neh-koo-tah'ah:

a. mesu–
    meh-soo–

b. kagitsuki
    kah-gee-tsoo-kee

c. osu–
    oh-soo–

d. pin–
    peen–

e. butai joo–
    boo-tye joh'oh–

f. chokusen ha
    choh-koo-sehn hah

g. san-shin
    sahn-sheen

h. ni-shin
    nee-sheen

i. kaiten kotei shiki
    kye-tehn koh-tay shee-kee

33. Denryuu:
    Dehn-r'yoo'oo:

a. tansoo
    tahn-soh'oh

b. sansoo
    sahn-soh'oh

34. Shadan Suicchi
    Shah-dahn Soo-eet-chee

35. Saikuru
    Sye-koo-roo

36. Dark

37. Dichroic

38. Diffusion

39. Diffusion-holder

40. Dimmer:

 a.   magnetic

 b.   reactance

 c.   resistance

 d.   thyristor

41. Dimmer Board

42. Direct Current (DC)

43. Distribution Box

44. Douser

45. Effects Light

46. Electricity

36. Kurai
    Koo-rye

37. Nishokusei
    Nee-shoh-koo-say

38. Kakusan
    Kah-koo-sahn

39. Kakusan Ban Hojiki
    Kah-koo-sahn Bahn Hoh-jee-kee

40. Chookooki:
    Choh'oh-koh'oh-kee:

   a.   jiki shiki
         jee-kee shee-kee

   b.   riakutansu gata
         ree-ah-koo-tahn-soo gah-tah

   c.   teikoo gata
         tay-koo gah-tah

   d.   sairisutaa
         sye-ree-soo-tah'ah

41. Chookooki Ban
    Choh'oh-koh'oh-kee Bahn

42. Chokuryuu
    Choh-koo-r'yoo'oo

43. Haiden Bako
    Hye-dehn Bah-koh

44. Supotto Raito Suicchi
    Soo-poht-toh Rye-toh Soo-eet-chee

45. Kooka no Aru Hikari
    Koh'oh-kah noh Ah-roo Hee-kah-ree

46. Denki
    Den-kee

47. Electrodes

48. Elevate

49. Ellipsoidal

50. Extension Wire

51. Eye-light

52. Feeder Cable

53. Ferrule Contact

54. Field

55. Filament

56. Fill-light

57. Filter

58. Flood

59. Fluorescent

60. Focus Knob

61. Follow-spot

47. Denkyoku
Dehn-k'yoh-koo

48. Mochiageru
Moh-chee-ah-geh-roo

49. Daenmen No
Dah-ehn-mehn Noh

50. Enchookee Buru
Ehn-choh'oh-keh'eh Boo-roo

51. Ai Raito
Eye Rye-toh

52. Fiidaa Sen
Fee'ee-dah'ah Sehn

53. Kuchigane Tsuki Setten
Koo-chee-gah-neh Tsoo-kee Seht-tehn

54. Fiirudo
Fee'ee-roo-doh

55. Firamento
Fee-rah-mehn-toh

56. Firu Raito
Fee-roo Rye-toh

57. Firutaa
Fee-roo-ṭah'ah

58. Tokoo
Toh-koh'oh

59. Keikoo
Kay-koh'oh

60. Fookasu Tsumami
Foh'oh-kah-soo Tsoo-mah-mee

61. Idoo Shiki Supotto Raito
Ee-doh Shee-kee Soo-poht-toh Rye-toh

62. Footcandle

63. Front-light

64. Frosted

65. Fuse

66. Fuse Box

67. Gelatine

68. Generator:

a.   gasoline

b.   diesel

69. Glass:

a.   silica

b.   quartz

70. Grid

71. Head

72. Hertz

62. Futto Kyandoru
    Foo't-toh K'yahn-doh-roo

63. Zenbu Raito
    Zen-boo Rye-toh

64. Tsuyakeshi
    Tsoo-yah-keh-shee

65. Hyuuzu
    H'yoo'oo-zoo

66. Hyuuzu Bako
    H'yoo'oo-zoo Bah-koh

67. Zerachin
    Zeh-rah-cheen

68. Hatsudenki:
    Hah-tsoo-dehn-kee:

 a.   gasorin enjin tsuki
       gah-soh-reen ehn-jeen tsoo-kee

 b.   diizeru enjin tsuki
       dee'ee-zeh-roo ehn-jeen tsoo-kee

69. Garasu:
    Gah-rah-soo:

 a.   shirika/keido
       shee-ree-kah/kay-doh

 b.   sekiei
       seh-kee-ay

70. Koshi
    Koh-shee

71. Heddo
    Hehd-doh

72. Herutsu
    Heh-roo-tsoo

73. High

74. High-key

75. HMI:

  a.   iodides

  b.   medium-arc

  c.   mercury

76. Ignition

77. Illumination

78. Incandescent

79. Insulation

80. Intensity

81. Jumper Cable

82. Key-light

83. "Kicker"

84. Kilowatt

73. Takai
    Tah-kye

74. Hai Kii
    Hye Kee'ee

75. HMI (Ecchi Emu Ai):
    HMI (Eh-chee Eh-moo Eye):

  a.   ionka
        ee-ohn-kah

  b.   chuukan no hono-o
        choo'oo-kahn noh hoh-noh-oh

  c.   suigen
        soo-ee-gehn

76. Tenka Soochi
    Tehn-kah Soh'oh-chee

77. Shoomei
    Shoh'oh-may

78. Hakunetsu Shita
    Hah-koo-neht-soo Shee-tah

79. Zetsuen
    Zeht-soo-ehn

80. Noodo
    Noh'oh-doh

81. Janpaa Sen
    Jahn-pah'ah Sehn

82. Kii Raito
    Kee'ee Rye-toh

83. Kage o Toru Hikari
    Kah-geh oh Toh-roo Hee-kah-ree

84. Kirowatto
    Kee-roh-waht-toh

85. Lamp

86. Lens:

a.   clear

b.   fresnel

c.   plano-convex

d.   step-

e.   diameter

f.   thickness

g.   focal point

87. Light:

a.   -stand

b.   -clamp

c.   balance

d.   -leak

e.   spill-

85. Denkyuu
    Den-k'yoo'oo

86. Renzu:
    Rehn-zoo:

a. heiman/furatto
   hay-mehn/foo-raht-toh

b. fureneru
   foo-reh-neh-roo

c. hei oo
   hye oh'oh

d. suteppu-
   soo-tehp-poo-

e. chokkukie
   Chohk-koo-ee-eh

f. -no atsumi
   -noh ah-tsoo-mee

g. -no shooten
   -noh shoh'oh-tehn

87. Hikari/Dentoo/Raito:
    Hee-kah-ree/Dehn-toh'oh/Rye-toh:

a. dentoo no dai
   dehn-toh'oh noh dye

b. dentoo yoo koteigu
   dehn-toh'oh yoh'oh koh-tay-goo

c. baransu
   bah-rahn-soo

d. hikari more
   kee-kah-ree moh-reh

e. zentai shoomei
   zen-tye shoh'oh-may

88. Lighting

89. Load

90. Load Calculation

91. Lock-knob

92. Lock Off

93. Low

94. Low-key

95. Lumen

96. Lumens-per-watt

97. Luminaire

98. Luminaire Ratings:

  a.   one hundred watt (100w)

  b.   two hundred watts (200w)

  c.   two hundred fifty watts (250w)

  d.   five hundred watts (500w)

88. Shoomei
    Shoh'oh-may

89. Fuka
    Foo-kah

90. Fuka Keisan
    Foo-kah Kay-sahn

91. Kotei Tsumami
    Koh-tay Tsoo-mah-mee

92. Kotei Suru
    Koh-tay Soo-roo

93. Hikui
    Hee-koo-ee

94. Teishoodo Shoomei
    Tay-shoh'oh-doh Shoh'oh-may

95. Ruumen
    Roo'oo-mehn

96. Ruumen/Watto
    Roo'oo-mehn/Waht-toh

97. Hakkoo
    Hahk-koh'oh

98. Hakkoo Kooritsu:
    Hahk-koh'oh Koh'oh-ree-tsoo:

  a. hyaku watto
      h'yah-koo what-toh

  b. nihyaku watto
      nee-h'yah-koo waht-toh

  c. nihyaku gojuu watto
      nee-h'yah-koo goh-joo'oo waht-toh

  d. gohyaku watto
      goh-h'yah-koo waht-toh

98. Luminaire Ratings (cont):

    e.   five-seventy-five watts (575w)

    f.   six hundred watts (600w)

    g.   six-fifty watts (650w)

    h.   seven-fifty watts (750w)

    i.   one thousand watts (1K)

    j.   two thousand watts (2K)

    k.   twenty-five hundred watts (2500w)

    l.   four thousand watts (4K)

    m.   five thousand watts (5K)

    n.   six thousand watts (6K)

    o.   ten thousand watts (10K)

 99. Luminous Flux

100. Lug

101. Lux

98. **Hakkoo Kooritsu (tsuzuku):**
    Hahk-koo Koh'oh-reet-soo (tsoo-zoo-koo):

   e. gohyaku nanajuu go watto
       goh-h'yah-koo nah-nah-joo'oo goh waht-
                                           toh

   f. roppyaku watto
       rohp-p'yah-koo waht-toh

   g. roppyaku gojuu watto
       rohp-p'yah-koo goh-joo'oo waht-toh

   h. nanahyaku gojuu watto
       nah-nah-h'yah-koo goh-joo waht-toh

   i. sen watto/ichi kiro watto
       sehn waht-toh/ee-chee kee-roh waht-toh

   j. nisen watto/ni kiro watto
       nee-sehn waht-toh/nee kee-roh waht-toh

   k. nisen gohyaku watto
       nee-sehn goh-h'yah-koo waht-toh

   l. yonsen watto/yon kiro watto
       yohn-sehn waht-toh/yohn kee-roh waht-toh

   m. gosen watto/go kiro watto
       goh-sehn waht-toh/goh kee-roh waht-toh

   n. rokusen watto/rokkiro watto
       roh-koo-sehn waht-toh/rohk-kee-roh waht-
                                              toh

   o. ichiman watto/jukkiro watto
       ee-chee-mahn waht-toh/jook-kee-roh waht-
                                              toh

99. **Kooryuu/Ruminasu Furakkasu**
    Koh'oh-r'yoo'oo/Roo-mee-nah-soo Foo-rahk-
                                          kah-soo

100. **Mini**
     Mee-nee

101. **Rukkusu**
     Rook-koo-soo

102. Mains

103. Meter:

  a.   am-

  b.   ohm-

  c.   volt-

104. Mercury Lamp

105. Metal Halide

106. Micro-switch

107. Net

108. Negative

109. Ohm

110. On/Off

111. Paddle

112. Pipe Grid

113. Plastic

102. Futoi Densen
     Foo-toy Den-sehn

103. Keiki/Meetaa:
     Kay-kee/Meh'eh-tah'ah:

   a.   denryuukei
        dehn-r'yoo'oo-kay

   b.   teikookei
        tay-koh'oh-kay

   c.   denatsukei
        dehn-ah-tsoo-kay

104. Suigintoo
     Soo-ee-geen-toh'oh

105. Haroogen Kinzoku
     Hah-roh'oh-gehn Keen-zoh-koo

106. Maikuro Suicchi
     Mye-koo-roh Soo-eet-chee

107. Koosen o Yawarageru
     Koh'oh-seh oh Yah-wah-rah-geh-roo

108. Fu
     Foo

109. Oomu
     Oh'oh-moo

110. On/Ofu
     Ohn/Oh-foo

111. Padoru Gata Konekutaa
     Pah-doh-roo Gah-tah Koh-neh-koo-tah'ah

112. Paipu Shiki Ranpu Hojiki
     Pye-poo Shee-kee Rahn-poo Hoh-jee-kee

113. Puransuchikku
     Poo-rahn-soo-cheek-koo

114. Plug

115. Plug-in Box

116. Positive

117. Power

118. Power Panel

119. Pre-focus

120. Primary

121. Receptacle

122. Rectifier

123. Reflector:

   a.   combination

   b.   ellipsoidal

   c.   parabolic

   d.   round

124. Regulator

114. Puragu
     Poo-rah-goo

115. Haiden Bako
     Hye-dehn Bah-koh

116. Sei
     Say

117. Chikara/Pawaa
     Chee-kah-rah/Pah-wah'ah

118. Seigyoban
     Say-g'yoh-bahn

119. Ranpu no Setto Appu
     Rahn-poo noh Seht-toh Ahp-poo

120. Ichiji
     Ee-chee-jee

121. Riseputakuru
     Ree-seh-poo-tah-koo-roo

122. Seiryuuki
     Say-r'yoo'oo-kee

123. Hanshaban:
     Hahn-shah-bahn:

   a.   kumiawase
        koo-mee-ah-wah-seh

   b.   daenkei
        dah-ehn-kay

   c.   parabora
        pah-rah-boh-rah

   d.   enkei
        ehn-kay

124. Chooseiki
     Choh'oh-say-kee

125. Rolling Stand

126. Scoop

127. Scrim:

   a.   single

   b.   double

   c.   triple

   d.   half-

   e.   quarter-

128. Secondary

129. Shadow

130. Short-circuit

131. Shutters

132. Side-light

133. Snoot

134. Socket Adapter

125. Sharintsuki Sutando
     Shah-reen-tsoo-kee S'tahn-doh

126. Oogata Raito
     Oh'oh-gah-tah Rye-toh

127. Ranpuno Maeni Tsukeru Ami:
     Rahn-poo-noh Mah-eh-nee Tsoo-keh-roo Ah-mee:

   a.   ichijuu/singuru
        ee-chee-joo'oo/seen-goo-roo

   b.   nijuu/daburu
        nee-joo'oo/dah-boo-roo

   c.   sanjuu
        sahn-joo'oo

   d.   hanbun
        hahn-boon

   e.   yonbun no ichi
        yohn-boon noh ee-chee

128. Niji
     Nee-jee

129. Kage
     Kah-geh

130. Tanraku
     Tahn-rah-koo

131. Shataa
     Shah-tah'ah

132. Yoko Raito
     Yoh-koh Rye-toh

133. Teepaatsuki Ranpu Ooi
     Teh'eh-pah'ah-tsoo-kee Rahn-poo Oh-oy

134. Soketta Adaputaa
     Soh-keht-tah Ah-dah-poo-tah'ah

135. Socket:

  a. single-ended

  b. double-ended

136. Sodium Vapor Lamp

137. Softlite

138. Spill-light

139. Spot

140. Stage Plug

141. Starter

142. Strand (wire)

143. Strip Light (ground row)

144. Sunlight

145. Switch:

  a. single-pole

  b. double-pole

135. Soketto:
    Soh-keht-toh:

   a. hitokuchi
       hee-toh-koo-chee

   b. futakuchi
       foo-tah-koo-chee

136. Natoryuumu
    Nah-toh-r'yoo'oo-moo

137. Yawarakai Shoomei
    Yah-wah-rah-kye Shoh'oh-may

138. Zentai no Shoomei
    Zen-tye noh Shoh'oh-may

139. Supotto Shoomei
    Soo-poht-toh Shoh'oh-may

140. Konsento
    Kohn-sehn-toh

141. Sutaataa
    Soo-tah'ah-tah'ah

142. Tanshin
    Tahn-sheen

143. Kogata Zentai Shoomei
    Koh-gah-tah Zen-tye Shoh'oh-may

144. Taiyoo Koo
    Tye-yoh'oh Koh'oh

145. Suicchi:
    Soo-eet-chee:

   a. ikkyoku
       eek-k'yoh-koo

   b. ni-kyoku
       nee-k'yoh-koo

146. Template

147. Terminals

148. Tilt:

  a. up

  b. down

149. Top-light

150. Tungsten-halogen

151. Transformer:

  a. step-down

  b. step-up

152. Vent

153. Voltage:

  a. high-

  b. low-

  c. one-hundred-ten

146. Idoo Yoo Dai
     Ee-doh'oh Yoh'oh Dye

147. Tanshi/Taaminaru
     Tahn-shee/Tah'ah-mee-nah-roo

148. Jooge Do:
     Joh'oh-geh Doh:

   a.   ue
        oo-eh

   b.   shita
        sh'tah

149. Joobu Raito
     Joh'oh-boo Rye-toh

150. Tangusuten Haroogen
     Tahn-goo-soo-tehn Hah-roh'oh-gehn

151. Toransu:
     Toh-rahn-soo:

   a.   kooka
        Koh'oh-kah

   b.   jooshoo
        joh'oh-shoh'oh

152. Ana
     Ah-nah

153. Denatsu:
     Deh-nah-tsoo:

   a.   takai-
        tah-kye-

   b.   hikui-
        hee-koo-ee-

   c.   hayaku juu
        hah-yah-koo joo'oo

153. Voltage (continued):

   d.   two-hundred-twenty

   e.   three-hundred-eighty

   f.   four-hundred-forty

154. Voltage Variation

155. Wire Mesh

156. Yoke

Useful Terms:

157. Danger: High Voltage

158. Do Not Touch

159. Do Not Use Metal Ladder

    In This Vicinity

160. Do Not Use On Electrical Fire

161. Man Working On Line

162. Warning: Not Grounded

153. Denatsu (tsuzuku):
     Dehn-ah-tsoo (tsoo-zoo-koo):

   d.   nihyaku nijuu
        nee-h'yah-koo nee-joo'oo

   e.   sanbyaku hachijuu
        sahn-b'yahk hah-chee-joo'oo

   f.   yonhyaku yonjuu
        yohn-h'yahk yohn-joo'oo

154. Denatsu Hendoo
     Dehn-ah-tsoo Hehn-doo

155. Amijoo Waiyaa
     Ah-mee-joh'oh Wye-yah'ah

156. Yooku
     Yoh'oh-koo

Yakunitatsu Kotoba:
Yahk-nee-tah-tsoo Koh-toh-bah:

157. Kiken: Koo Denatsu
     Kee-kahn: Koh'oh Dehn-ah-tsoo

158. Sawaruna!
     Sah-wah-roo-nah!

159. Kono Chikakude Kinzokusei
     Koh-noh Chee-kah-koo-deh Keen-zoh-koo-
                                          say

     Hashigo o Tsukauna!
     Hah-shee-goh oh Tsoo-k'ow'nah!

160. Denki Kasai Niwa Tsukauna!
     Den-kee Kah-sye Nee-wah Tsoo-k'ow-nah!

161. Koojichuu
     Koh'oh-jee-choo'oo

162. Keikoku: Aasu Nashi
     Kay-koh-koo: Ah'ah-soo Nah-shee

01. Absorption

02. Achromatic

03. Additive

04. After Image

05. Antihalation

06. Backing

07. Black and White (B&W)

08. Bleach

09. Blow-up

10. Blur

11. Can

12. Characteristic Curve (d log e):

a.   shoulder

b.   straight line portion of curve

c.   toe

FUIRUMU 65
FOO-EE-ROO-MOO

01. Kyuushuu
    K'yoo'oo-shoo'oo

02. Nishokusei
    Nee-shoh-koo-say

03. Shikiryoo no San Genshoku
    Shee-keer'yoh'oh noh Sahn Gehn-shoh-koo

04. Zanzoo
    Zahn-zoh'oh

05. Hareeshon Booshi
    Hah-reh'eh-shohn Boh'oh-shee

06. Bakkingu
    Bahk-keen-goo

07. Kuro Shiro
    Koo-roh Shee-roh

08. Kajoo Rokoo
    Kah-joh'oh Roh-koh'oh

09. Hikinobashi
    Hee-kee-noh-bah-shee

10. Boke
    Boh-keh

11. Kan Iri
    Kahn Ee-ree

12. Seinoo Kyokusen
    Say-noh'oh K'oh-koo-sehn

   a. kata bubun
    kah-tah boo-boon

   b. chokusen bubun
    choh-koo-sehn boo-boon

   c. tachiagari bubun
    tah-chee-ah-gah-ree boo-boon

13. Cinch Marks

14. Clarity

15. Code Numbers

16. Color:

 a.   blue

 b.   cyan

 c.   green

 d.   magenta

 e.   red

 f.   yellow

 g.   white

17. Color Couplers

18. Color Film

19. Color Temperature

20. Composite Daily

13. Shinchi Maaku
    Sheen-chee Mah'ah-koo

14. Toomeido
    Toh'oh-may-doh

15. Koodo Nanbaa
    Koh'oh-doh Nahn-bah'ah

16. Iro:
    Ee-roh:

  a. ao
      ah-oh

  b. shian
      shee-ahn

  c. midori
      mee-doh-ree

  d. mazenda
      mah-zen-dah

  e. aka
      ah-kah

  f. ki
      kee

  g. shiro
      shee-roh

17. Hasshoku Zai
    Hahs-shoh-koo Zye

18. Karaa Fuirumu
    Kah-rah'ah Foo-ee-roo-moo

19. Iro Ondo
    Ee-roh Ohn-doh

20. Onsei Henshuu Sareteinai Fuirumu
    Ohn-say Hehn-shoo Sah-reh-tay-nye Foo-ee-
    roo-moo

21. Contrast

22. Contrast Range

23. Core

24. Darkroom

25. Daylight Film

26. Defect

27. Deficient

28. Detail

29. Density

30. Densitometer

31. Desaturate

32. Develop:

  a.   force one-stop

  b.   force two-stops

  c.   normal

21. Kontorasuto
    Kohn-toh-rah-soo-toh

22. Kontorasuto Renji
    Kohn-toh-rah-soo-toh Rehn-jee

23. Chuushin
    Choo'oo-sheen

24. Anshitsu
    Ahn-shee-tsoo

25. Hiruma Yoo Fuirumu
    Hee-roo-mah Yoh'oh Foo-ee-roo-mah

26. Ketten
    Keht-tehn

27. Ketten no Aru
    Keht-tehn noh Ah-roo

28. Saibu
    Sye-boo

29. Noodo
    Noh'oh-doh

30. Noodokei
    Noh'oh-doh-kay

31. Shiroppoku
    Shee-rohp-poh-koo

32. Genzoo:
    Gehn-zoh'oh:

  a. ichidan henkoo
      ee-chee-dahn hehn-koh'oh

  b. nidan henkoo
      nee-dahn hehn-koh'oh

  c. tsuujoo
      tsoo'oo-joh'oh

33. Dirt

34. Dye

35. Dupe Negative

36. Edge Number

37. Effluent

38. Emulsion

39. Exposure:

a.   over-exposed

b.   under-exposed

40. Exposure Index

41. Exposure Range

42. Film

43. Filter

44. Fine Grain

45. Fixer

33. Yogore
    Yoh-goh-reh

34. Senryo
    Sehn-r'yoh

35. Dyuupu Sareta Nega
    D'yoo'oo-poo Sah-reh-tah Neh-gah

36. Ejji Nanbaa
    Ehj-jee Nahn-bah'ah

37. Genzoo Haikei
    Gehn-zoh'oh Hye-kay

38. Nyuuzai
    N'yoo'oo-zye

39. Roshutsu:
    Roh-shoo-tsoo:

  a.　rokoo oobaa
      roh-koh'oh oh'oh-bah'ah

  b.　rokoo andaa
      roh-koh'oh ahn-dah'ah

40. Rokoo Shisuu
    Roh-koh'oh Shee-soo'oo

41. Rokoo Renji
    Roh-koh'oh Rehn-jee

42. Fuirumu
    Foo-ee-roo-moo

43. Firutaa
    Fee-roo-tah'ah

44. Biryuushi
    Bee-r'yoo'oo-shee

45. Teichaku Eki
    Tay-chah-koo Eh-kee

46. Flash:

a. post-

b. pre-

47. Flat

48. Flesh Tone

49. Fog:

a. edge-

b. full-frame-

50. Frame

51. Frameline

52. Gamma

53. Generation:

a. first

b. second

c. third

46. Suisen:
    Soo-ee-sehn:

  a.   ato
     ah-toh

  b.   mae
     mah-eh

47. Taira
    Tye-rah

48. Furesshu Toon
    Foo-rehs-shoo Toh'ohn

49. Kiri:
    Kee-ree:

  a.   sumi-
     soo-mee-

  b.   zentai-
     zen-tye-

50. Fureemu/Waku
    Foo-reh'eh-moo/Wah-koo

51. Fureemu Rain
    Foo-reh'eh-moo Rye'n

52. Ganma
    Gahn-mah

53. Sedai:
    Seh-dye:

  a.   dai-ichi
     dye-ee-chee

  b.   dai-ni
     dye-nee

  c.   dai-san
     dye-sahn

54. Grey Scale

55. Grain

56. Granularity

57. High-contrast-positive

58. Highlight

59. Hue

60. Identification Label

61. Infra-red

62. Intermediate

63. Internegative

64. Kelvin Scale

65. Laboratory

66. Latent Image

67. Latitude

68. Light Leak

54. Gurei Sukeeru
    Goo-ray Soo-keh-roo

55. Gein
    Gayn

56. Ryuujoosei
    R'yoo'oo-joh'oh-say

57. Koo Kontorasuto Poji
    Koh'oh Kohn-toh-rah-soo-toh Poh-jee

58. Hairaito
    Hye-rye-toh

59. Iroai
    Ee-roh-eye

60. Shikibetsu Raberu
    Shee-kee-beh-tsoo Rah-beh-roo

61. Sekigaisen
    Seh-kee-gye-sehn

62. Chuukan
    Choo'oo-kahn

63. Nega Kara Totta Nega
    Neh-gah Kah-rah Toht-tah Neh-gah

64. Kerubin Sukeeru
    Keh-roo-been Soo-keh'eh-roo

65. Genzoojyo
    Gehn-zoh'oh-j'yoh

66. Senzoo
    Sehn-zoh'oh

67. Rachichuudo
    Rah-chee-choo'oo-doh

68. Hikari More
    Hee-kah-ree Moh-reh

69. Light Struck

70. Magnetic-striped

71. Motion Picture Film

72. Negative

73. Opaque

74. Original

75. Perforation:

  a.   double-

  b.   single-

76. Pitch:

  a.   long

  b.   short

77. Print:

  a.   answer

  b.   contact

69. Hikari More
    Hee-kah-ree Moh-reh

70. Jiki Sutoraipu
    Jee-kee S'toh-rye-poo

71. Eiga Yoo Fuirumu
    Ay-gah Yoh'oh Foo-ee-roo-mah

72. Nega
    Neh-gah

73. Futoomei
    Foo-toh'oh-may

74. Orijinaru
    Oh-ree-jee-nah-roo

75. Paaforeeshon:
    Pah'ah-foh-reh'eh-shohn:

   a. ryoogawa-
       r'yoh'oh-gah-wah-

   b. katagawa-
       kah-tah-gah-wah-

76. Picchi:
    Peet-chee:

   a. nagai
       nah-gye

   b. mijikai
       mee-jee-kye

77. Purinto:
    Poo-reen-toh:

   a. saishuu kakunin yoo
       sye-shoo'oo kah-koo-neen yoh'oh

   b. micchaku
       meet-chah-koo

77. Print (continued):

c. corrected (timed)

d. one-light

e. optical

f. positive

g. release

78. Print Down

79. Print-scale

80. Print Up

81. Printer-light

82. Rawstock

83. Reciprocity

84. Reduction

85. Resolution

86. Response

77. Purinto (tsuzuku):
    Poo-reen-toh (tsoo-zoo-koo):

  c.   rokoo hosei zumi
        roh-koh'oh hoh-say zoo-mee

  d.   tanitsukoo
        tan-ee-tsoo-koh'oh

  e.   koogaku shiki
        koh'oh-gah-koo shee-kee

  f.   poji
        poh-jee

  g.   happyoo yoo
        hahp-p'yoh'oh yoh'oh

78. Kuraku Purinto Suru
    Koo-rah-koo Poo-reen-toh Soo-roo

79. Purinto Sukeero
    Poo-reen-toh Soo-keh'eh-roh

80. Akaruku Purinto Suru
    Ah-kah-roo-koo Poo-reen-toh Soo-roo

81. Purinto Yoo Koogen
    Poo-reen-toh Yoh'oh Koh'oh-gehn

82. Misatsuei Fuirumu
    Mee-sah-tsoo-ay Foo-ee-roo-moo

83. Soogo Sayoo
    Soh'oh-goh Sah-yoh'oh

84. Shukushoo
    Shoo-koo-shoh'oh

85. Kaizoo Ryoku
    Kye-zoh'oh R'yoh-koo

86. Han-noo
    Hahn-noh'oh

87. Reversal

88. Rushes

89. Saturation

90. Scratch

91. Sensitivity

92. Shadow

93. Sharpness

94. Silent

95. Silver

96. Solution (liquid)

97. Sound

98. Spool

99. Stain

100. Step-print

101. Still Photograph

87. Ribaasaru
    Ree-bah'ah-sah-roo

88. Shitami Yoo Purinto
    Shee-tah-mee Yoh'oh Poo-reen-toh

89. Hoowa
    Hoh'oh-wah

90. Kizu
    Kee-zoo

91. Kando
    Kahn-doh

92. Kage
    Kah-geh

93. Sen-eido
    Sehn-ay-doh

94. Musei
    Moo-say

95. Gin
    Geen

96. Yooeki
    Yoh'oh-kee

97. Onsei
    Ohn-say

98. Supuuru
    Soo-poo'oo-roo

99. Yogore
    Yoh-goh-reh

100. Hitokoma Gotono Purinto
     Hee-toh-koh-mah Goh-toh-noh Poo-reen-toh

110. Suchiiru Shashin
     Soo-chee'ee-roo Shah-sheen

102. Subtractive

103. Test-strip

104. Tone

105. Tungsten Film

106. Ultra-violet

107. Visible Spectrum

108. Wash

109. Water

110. Wavelength

<u>Useful Terms</u>:

111. Keep From Radiation

112. Open In Darkness Only

113. Do Not Expose To Light

114. Darkroom In Use

115. Darkroom: Keep Out

102. Shikikoo no Sangenshoku
 Shee-kee-koh'oh noh Sahn-gehn-shoh-koo

103. Rokoo Chooseiyoo Fuirumu
 Roh-koh'oh Choh'oh-say-yoh'oh Foo-ee-roo
 -moo

104. Toon
 Toh'ohn

105. Tangusuten Raitoyoo Fuirumu
 Tahn-goo-soo-tehn Rye-toh-yoh'oh Foo-ee-
 roo-moo

106. Shigaisen
 Shee-gye-sen

107. Kashikoo Supekutoramu
 kah-shee-koh'oh Soo-peh-koo-toh-rah-moo

108. Suisen
 Soo-ee-sehn

109. Mizu
 Mee-zoo

110. Hachoo
 Hah-choh'oh

Yakunitatsu Kotoba:
Yahk-nee-tah-tsoo Koh-toh-bah:

111. Hooshasen Hibaku Fuka
 Hoh'oh-shah-sehn Hee-bah-koo Foo-kah

112. Ansho Kaifuu
 Ahn-shoh Kye-foo'oo

113. Hikari Ni Ateruna
 Hee-kah-ree Nee Ah-teh-roo-nah

114. Anshitsu Shiyoochuu
 Ahn-shee-tsoo Shee-yoh'oh-choo'oo

115. Anshitsu: Tachiiri Kinshi
 Ahn-shee-tsoo: Tah-chee'ee-ree Keen-shee

01. Apple Box

02. Backing

03. Bar Clamp

04. Bazooka

05. Black Cloth

06. Blade

07. Breakaway

08. Butterfly

09. Camera Mount

10. Car Mount

11. C-clamp

12. Chain

13. "Cookie"

14. Crane

15. Cukaloris

01. Doogu Ire
    Doh'oh-goo Ee-reh

02. Urauchi
    Oo-r'ow-chee

03. Boo Dome
    Boh'oh Doh-meh

04. Bazuuka
    Bah-zoo'oo-kah

05. Kuro Nuno
    Koo-roh Noo-noh

06. Ha
    Hah

07. Bunri
    Boon-ree

08. Oogata Netto
    Oh'oh-gah-tah Neht-toh

09. Kamera Maunto
    Kah-meh-rah M'ow'n-toh

10. Jidoosah Maunto
    Jee-doh'oh-sah M'ow'n-toh

11. Kuranpu
    Koo-rahn-poo

12. Kusari
    Koo-sah-ree

13. Kage o Tsukuru Ita
    Kah-geh o Tsoo-koo-roo Ee-tah

14. Kureen
    Koo-reh'en

15. Kage o Tsukuru Ita
    Kah-geh oh Tsoo-koo-roo Ee-tah

16. Cutter

17. Cup Block

18. Cyclorama

19. Diffusion

20. Director's Chair

21. Dolly:

 a. boards

 b. track

 c. curved

 d. section

 e. straight

22. Doorway Dolly

23. Dot

24. Drapery

25. Dulling Spray

16. Kattaa
    Kaht-tah'ah

17. Sharin no Kaitendome
    Shah-reen noh Kye-tehn-doh-meh

18. Sora no Bakku
    Soh-rah noh Bahk-koo

19. Kakusan
    Kah-koo-sahn

20. Direkutaa no Isu
    Dee-reh-koo-tah'ah no Ee-soo

21. Doorii:
    Doh'oh-ree'ee:

  a.   ita
     ee-tah

  b.   reeru
     reh'eh-roo

  c.   magatta
     mah-gaht-tah

  d.   reeru no bubun
     reh'roo noh boo-boon

  e.   massuguna
     mahs-soo-goo-nah

22. Doa o Tooru
    Doh-ah oh Toh'oh-roo

23. Ten
    Tehn

24. Kaaten
    Kah'ah-tehn

25. Hanshadome Supurei
    Hahn-shah-doh-meh Soo-poo-ray

26. Elevator

27. Extension-arm

28. Flag

29. Flexible-arm

30. Foil

31. Furniture Pad

32. Grid

33. Grip-clip

34. Grip-kit

35. Grip Stand

36. Gobo

37. Half-apple Box

38. Hanger

39. High-stand

40. Holder

26. Erebeetaa
    Eh-reh-beh'eh-tah'ah

27. Enchoo Aamu
    Ehn-choh'oh Ah'ah-moo

28. Shako Maku
    Shah-koh Mah-koo

29. Jizai Aamu
    Jee-zye Ah'ah-moo

30. Hoiru
    Hoy-roo

31. Kagu Yoo Kusshon
    Kah-goo Yoh'oh Koos-shohn

32. Kooshi
    Koh'oh-shee

33. Oogata Kurippu
    Oh'oh-gah-tah Koo-reep-poo

34. Kotei Yoogubako
    Koh-tay Yoh'oh-goo-bah-koh

35. Sutando
    Soo-tahn-doh

36. Shakooban
    Shah-koh'oh-bahn

37. Chuugata Doogu-ire
    Choo'oo-gah-tah Doh'oh-goo-ee-reh

38. Hangaa
    Hahn-gah'ah

39. Takai Sutando
    Tah-kye Soo-tahn-doh

40. Horudaa
    Hoh-roo-dah'ah

41. Ladder

42. Lockdown Knob

43. Low Stand

44. Meat-axe

45. Metal Frame

46. Net:

   a. open-end

   b. open-side

   c. closed-end

47. Offset-arm

48. Overhead

49. Pancake

50. Parallel

51. Pipe Clamp

52. Pipe Frame

41. Hashigo
    Hah-shee-goh

42. Shimetsuke Nobu
    Shee-meht-soo-keh Noh-boo

43. Hikui Sutando
    Hee-koo-ee Soo-tahn-doh

44. Ono
    Oh-noh

45. Kinzoku Fuirumu
    Keen-zoh-koo Foo-ee-roo-moo

46. Ami:
    Ah-mee:

   a. kuchi no aita
       koo-chee noh eye-tah

   b. yoko no aita
       yoh-koh noh eye-tah

   c. kuchi no fusagatta
       koo-chee noh foo-sah-gaht-tah

47. Katayori Boo
    Kah-tah-yoh-ree Boh'oh

48. Zujoo
    Zoo-joh'oh

49. Kogata Doogu-ire
    Koh-gah-tah Doh'oh-goo-ee-reh

50. Heikoo
    Hay-koh'oh

51. Paipu Dome
    Pye-poo Doh-meh

52. Paipu Fureemu
    Pye-poo Foo-reh'eh-moo

53. Platform

54. Rails

55. Raincover

56. Reflector:

  a.   gold

  b.   hard-side

  c.   scattered

  d.   silver

  e.   soft-side

  f.   specular

  g.   stand

  h.   yoke

  i.   leaf

57. (to) Rig

58. Rigging

53. Dai
    Dye

54. Reeru
    Reh'eh-roo

55. Ame Yoke Kabaa
    Ah-meh Yoh-keh Kah-bah'ah

56. Rifurekutaa:
    Ree-foo-reh-koo-tah'ah:

   a.   kin no
        keen noh

   b.   hyoomen no katai
        h'yoh'oh-mehn noh kah-tye

   c.   mabarana
        mah-bah-rah-nah

   d.   gin no
        geen noh

   e.   hyoomen no yawarakai
        h'yoh'oh-mehn noh yah-wah-rah-kye

   f.   kyoomen no
        k'yoh'oh-mehn noh

   g.   sutando
        soo-tahn-doh

   h.   wai gata hojiki
        wye gah-tah hoh-jee-kee

   i.   kogata arumihaku
        koh-gah-tah ah-roo-mee-hah-koo

57. Yooisuru
    Yoh'oy-soo-roo

58. Yooi
    Yoh-oy

59. Riser

60. Rope

61. Safety Line

62. Scaffold

63. Scenery

64. Scenic Flat

65. Scrim

66. Shim

67. Show Card

68. Side-arm

69. Silk

70. Skyhook

71. Solid

72. Target

73. Teaser

59. Mochiage Kanage
    Moh-chee-ah-geh Kah-nah-geh

60. Roopu
    Roh'oh-poo

61. Anzen Roopu
    Ahn-zen Roh'oh-poo

62. Ashiba
    Ah-shee-bah

63. Kakiwari
    Kah-kee-wah-ree

64. Haikei
    Hye-kay

65. Ami
    Ah-mee

66. Kusabi
    Koo-sah-bee

67. Aizu Yoo Kaado
    Eye-zoo Yoh'oh Kah'ah-doh

68. Yokogi
    Yoh-koh-gee

69. Kinu
    Kee-noo

70. Hukku
    Hoo'k-koo

71. Katai
    Kah-tye

72. Taagetto
    Tah'ah-geh'eht-toh

73. Shokaiyoo Fuirumu
    Shoh-kye-yoh'oh Foo-ee-roo-moo

74. Telescopic

75. Trapeze

76. Trombone

77. Tubing

78. Umbrella

79. Wallsled

80. Wedge

81. "Wild"-wall

Useful Terms:

82. Hot Set

83. Keep Clear

84. Keep Off

85. Nail it!

86. Set Brake

87. That's Good!

74. Shinshuku Jizai no
    Sheen-shoo-koo Jee-zye noh

75. Buranko
    Boo-rahn-koh

76. Shinshuku Jizai no
    Sheen-shoo-koo Jee-zye noh

77. Paipu Zairyoo
    Pye-poo Zye-r'yoh'oh

78. Kasa
    Kah-sah

79. Idooshiki Kabe
    Ee-doh'oh-shee-kee Kah-beh

80. Kusabi
    Koo-sah-bee

81. Idooshiki Kabe
    Ee-doh'oh-shee-kee Kah-beh

Yakunitatsu Kotoba:
Yahk-nee-tah-tsoo Koh-toh-bah:

82. Kimatta Setto
    Kee-maht-tah Seht-toh

83. Setto Ni Sawaruna
    Seht-toh Nee Sah-wah-roo-nah

84. Tachiiri Kinshi
    Tah-chee'ee-ree Keen-shee

85. Kugide Ute!
    Koo-gee-deh Oo-teh!

86. Setto o Koteiseyo
    Seht-toh oh Koh-tay-seh-yoh

87. Korewa Yoi!
    Koh-reh-wah Yoy!

Useful Terms (continued):

88. Watch Your Head

89. Wear a Hardhat

90. Wear Protective Glasses

91. Just a little more!

92. Too Much!

93. Just a Little Less

94. To the Left

95. To the Right

<u>Yakunitatsu Kotoba (tsuzuku)</u>:
Yahk-nee-tah-tsoo Koh-toh-bah (tsoo-soo-koo):

88. Zujoo Chuui
    Zoo-joh'oh Choo'oo-ee

89. Herumetto Chakuyoo
    Heh-roo-meht-toh Chah-koo-yoh'oh

90. Hogo Megane Chakuyoo
    Hoh-goh Meh-gah-neh Chah-koo-yoh'oh

91. Moo-sukoshi Ooku
    Moh'oh-s'koh-shee Oh'oh-koo

92. Oo-sugiru
    Oh'oh-soo-gee-roo

93. Moo-sukoshi Sukunakie
    Moh'oh-s'koh-shee S'koo-nah-kee-eh

94. Hidari Ni/Hidari E
    Hee-dah-ree Nee/Hee-dah-ree Eh

95. Migi Ni/Migi E
    Mee-gee Nee/Mee-gee Eh

01. Ambience

02. Amplifier

03. Amplitude Modulation (AM)

04. Attenuation

05. Audio

06. Automatic-level-control

07. Background Noise

08. Baffle

09. Balance

10. Bass

11. Batteries

12. Boom (equipment)

13. Boom (hollow sound)

14. Bridge

15. Bulk Eraser

01. Enshuu
    Ehn-shoo'oo

02. Zoofukuki
    Zoh'oh-foo-koo-kee

03. Shinpuku Henchoo
    Sheen-poo-koo   Hehn-choh'oh

04. Gensui
    Gehn-soo-ee

05. Oto/Oodio
    Oh-toh/Oh'oh-dee-oh

06. Jidoo Reberu Contorooru
    Jee-doh'oh Reh-beh-roo Kohn-toh-roh'oh-roo

07. Haikei Noizu
    Hye-kay Noy-zu

08. Onkyoo Booshi Soochi
    Ohn-k'yoh'oh Boh'oh-shee Soh'oh-chee

09. Baransu
    Bah-rahn-soo

10. Teion
    Tay-ohn

11. Batterii/Denchi
    Baht-teh-ree'ee/Den-chee

12. Hari
    Hah-ree

13. Buun On
    Boo'oon Ohn

14. Hashi
    Hah-shee

15. Shookyo Soochi
    Shoh'oh-k'yoh Soh'oh-chee

16. Cable

17. Capstan

18. Cassette

19. Change Tape

20. Channel

21. Circuit

22. Cleaner

23. Commentary

24. Composite

25. Connector

26. Console

27. Contacts

28. Cross-cut

29. Cross-fade

30. Cue

16. Keeburu
    Keh'eh-boo-roo

17. Kyapusutan
    K'yah-poo-soo-tahn

18. Kasetto
    Kah-seht-toh

19. Teepu o Kaeru
    Teh'eh-poo oh Kah-eh-roo

20. Chan-neru
    Chahn-neh-roo

21. Kairo
    Kye-roh

22. Kuriinaa
    Koo-ree'ee-nah'ah

23. Kiroku
    Kee-roh-koo

24. Goosei
    Goh'oh-say

25. Konekutaa
    Koh-neh-koo-tah'ah

26. Konsooru
    Kohn-soh'oh-roo

27. Kontakuto
    Kohn-tah-koo-toh

28. Shin no Koogo Irekae
    Sheen noh Koh'oh-goh Ee-reh-kah-eh

29. Koogo Feido
    Koh'oh-goh Fay-doh

30. Aizu
    Eye-zoo

31. Crystal Control

32. Decibel

33. Degauss

34. Dialogue

35. Distortion

36. Double System

37. Dual Track

38. Dub

39. Dubbing

40. Dupe

41. Effects

42. Electronics

43. Equalize

44. Extension

45. Fade-in

31. Kurisutaru Kontorooru
    Koo-ree-soo-tah-roo Kohn-toh-roh'oh-roo

32. Deshiberu
    Deh-shee-beh-roo

33. Haijitai
    Hye-jee-tye

34. Kaiwa/Daiarogu
    Kye-wah/Dye-ah-roh-goo

35. Yugami
    Yoo-gah-mee

36. Daburu Shisutemu
    Dah-boo-roo Shee-soo-teh-moo

37. Nijuu no
    Nee-joo'oo noh

38. Sai Rukuon
    Sye Roo-koo-ohn

39. Dabingu
    Dah-been-goo

40. Dyuupu
    D'yoo'oo-poo

41. Kooka
    Koh'oh-kah

42. Denshi
    Den-shee

43. Heikinka Suru
    Hay-keen-kah Soo-roo

44. Enchoo
    Ehn-choo

45. Feido In
    Fay-doh Een

46. Fade-out

47. Fidelity

48. Final Mix

49. Fishpole (hand-held boom)

50. Flutter

51. Frequency:

 a.   high-

 b.   low-

52. Frequency Modulation (FM)

53. Frequency Response

54. Generator

55. Headphones

56. Hum

57. Inches-per-second

58. Input

46. Feido Auto
    Fay-doh Ow'toh

47. Chuujitsudo
    Choo'oo-jee-tsoo-doh

48. Saishuu Mikkusu
    Sye-shoo'oo Meek-koo-soo

49. Temochi no Boo
    Teh-moh-chee noh Boh'oh

50. Saisei Mura
    Sye-say Moo-rah

51. Shuuhasuu:
    Shoo'oo-hah-soo'oo:

  a.   takai-
        tah-kye-

  b.   hikui-
        hee-koo-ee-

52. Shuuhasuu Henchoo
    Shoo'oo-hah-soo'oo Hehn-choh'oh

53. Shuuhasuu Risuponsu
    Shoo'oo-hah-soo'oo Ree-soo-pohn-soo

54. Hatsudenki
    Hah-tsoo-den-kee

55. Heddohon
    Hehd-doh-hohn

56. Hamu On
    Hah-moo Ohn

57. Inchi/Byo
    Een-chee/B'yoh

58. Nyuuryoku/Inputto
    N'yoo'oo-r'yoh-koo/Een-poot-toh

59. Interlock

60. Interview

61. Iron-oxide

62. Jack

63. Laydown

64. Lead-in

65. Lip-sync

66. (to) Loop

67. Looping

68. Loud

69. Lower Register

70. Maintenance

71. Magnetic Stock:

a.   fullcoat

b.   striped

59. Intaarokku
    Een-tah'ah-rohk-koo

60. Intabyuu
    Een-tah-b'yoo'oo

61. Sankatetsu
    Sahn-kah-teh-tsoo

62. Jyakku
    J'yahk-koo

63. Genzoogo no Onsei Soonyuu
    Gehn-zoh'oh-goh noh Ohn-say Soh'oh-n'yoc'
    oo

64. Hikikomi
    Hee-kee-koh-mee

65. Rippu Shinku
    Reep-poo Sheen-koo

66. Tsunagi Awaseta Fuirumu/Teepu
    Tsoo-nah-gee Ah-wah-seh-tah Foo-ee-roo-
    moo/Teh'eh-poo

67. Ruupingu
    Roo'oo-peen-goo

68. Oogoe
    Oh'oh-goh-eh

69. Tei-oniki
    Tay-oh-nee-kee

70. Hoshuu
    Hoh-shoo

71. Jikizairyoo:
    Jee-kee-zye-r'yoh'oh:

  a.   zenmen kooto
        zen-mehn koh'oh-toh

  b.   sutoraipu
        soo-toh-rye-poo

72. Magnetic Transfer

73. Master

74. Microphone:

  a.   bidirectional

  b.   directional

  c.   condenser

  d.   hand

  e.   lapel

  f.   lavalier

  g.   non-directional

  h.   omni-directional

  i.   shotgun

  j.   uni-directional

  k.   wireless

75. Microphone Lines

72. Jikitensha
    Jee-kee-tehn-shah

73. Masutaa
    Mah-soo-tah'ah

74. Maikurohon:
    Mye-koo-roh-hohn:

  a. soo hookoosei
     soh'oh hoh'oh-koh'oh-say

  b. shikoosei
     shee-koh'oh-say

  c. kondensaa
     kohn-dehn-sah'ah

  d. temochi no-
     teh-moh-chee noh-

  e. eri ni tsukeru-
     eh-ree nee tsoo-keh-roo-

  f. eri ni tsukeru-
     eh-ree nee tso-keh-roo-

  g. mushikoosei no-
     moo-shee-koh'oh-say noh-

  h. zen hookoosei no-
     zen hoh'oh-koh'oh say noh-

  i. shottogan gata no-
     shoht-toh-gahn gah-tah noh-

  j. shikoosei
     shee-koh-say

  k. waiyaresu
     wye-yah-reh-soo

75. Maiku Koodo
    Mye-koo Koh'oh-doh

76. Mid-range

77. Mix

78. Mix-down

79. Mix Panel

80. Modulated:

a.   over-

b.   under-

81. Monaural

82. Multiple Track

83. Music

84. Musical Score

85. Narration

86. Noise:

a.   high-

b.   low-

76. Chuu-oniki
    Choo'oo-ohn-ee-kee

77. Mikkusu
    Meek-koo-soo

78. Mikkusu
    Meek-koo-soo

79. Mikisaa Paneru
    Mee-kee-sah'ah Pah-neh-roo

80. Henchoo:
    Hehn-choh'oh:

 a. -kata
    -kah-tah

 b. -kashoo
    -kah-shoh'oh

81. Monoraru
    Moh-noh-rah-roo

82. Tasuu Torakku
    Tah-soo'oo Toh-rahk-koo

83. Ongaku
    Ohn-gah-koo

84. Gakufu
    Gah-koo-foo

85. Nareeshon
    Nah-reh'eh-shohn

86. Zatsuon:
    Zah-tsoo-ohn:

 a. takai
    tah-kye

 b. hikui
    hee-koo-ee

87. Optical:

a.   stock

b.   track

c.   transfer

88. Oscillator

89. Out-of-sync

90. Ouput

91. Peak

92. Pick-up

93. Pin

94. Playback Head

95. Plug

96. Post-production Mix

97. Post-synchronize

98. Potentiometer

87. Koogaku Shiki:
    Koh'oh-gah-koo Shee-kee:

   a. fuirumu rui
       foo-ee-roo-moo roo-ee

   b. torakku
       toh-rahk-koo

   c. tensha
       tehn-shah

88. Hasshinki
    Hahs-sheen-kee

89. Hi-doochoo
    Hee-doh'oh-choh'oh

90. Shitsuryoku
    Shee-tsoo-r'yoh-koo

91. Piiku
    Pee'ee-koo

92. Pikku Appu
    Peek-koo Ahp-poo

93. Pin
    Peen

94. Saisei Heddo
    Sye-say Hehd-doh

95. Puragu
    Poo-rah-goo

96. Ato Mikkusu
    Ah-toh Meek-koo-soo

97. Ato Shinku
    Ah-toh Sheen-koo

98. Pootensho-meetaa
    Poh'oh-tehn-shoh-meh'eh-tah'ah

99. Power Consumption

100. Pre-amplifier

101. Public Address System

102. Quality

103. Range

104. Receiver

105. Receptacle

106. Record (noun)

107. Record (adj)

108. Recorded Tape

109. Recording Channel

110. Recording Head

111. Reel

112. Reel-to-reel

113. Re-record

99. Shoohi Denryoku
    Shoh'oh-hee Den-r'yoh-koo

100. Puri Anpu
     Poo-ree Ahn-poo

101. Kakusei Soochi
     Kah-koo-say Soh'oh-chee

102. Shitsu
     Shee-tsoo

103. Renji
     Rehn-jee

104. Reshiibaa
     Reh-she'ee-bah'ah

105. Riseputakuru
     Ree-seh-poo-tah-koo-roo

106. Rokuon
     Roh-koo-ohn

107. Kirokusuru/Rokuonsuru
     Kee-roh-koo-soo-roo/Roh-koo-ohn-soo-roo

108. Rokuon Teepu
     Roh-koo-ohn Teh'eh-poo

109. Rokuon Channeru
     Roh-koo-ohn Chahn-neh-roo

110. Rokuon Heddo
     Roh-koo-ohn Hehd-doh

111. Riiru
     Ree'ee-roo

112. Riiru Kara Riiru E
     Ree'ee-roo Kah-rah Ree'ee-roo Eh

113. Sai-rokuon
     Sye-roh-koo-ohn

114. Resolver

115. Re-wind

116. Room Tone

117. Rustle

118. Rhythmic

119. Scene

120. Scratch Track

121. Shielded Wire

122. Sibilants

123. Single-track

124. Single-system

125. Smooth

126. Soft

127 Solid State

114. Kyoowa Soochi
K'yoh'oh-wah Soh'oh-chee

115. Makimodoshi
Mah-kee-moh-doh-shee

116. Shitsunai Onkyoo
Shee-tsoo-nye Ohn-k'yoh'oh

117. Sarasara-on
Sah-rah-sah-rah-ohn

118. Rizumikaru
Ree-zoo-mee-kah-roo

119. Shiin
Shee'een

120. Sagyoo Saundo Torakku
Sah-g'yoh'oh S'ow'n-doh Toh-rahk-koo

121. Shiirudosen
Shee'ee-roo-doh-sehn

122. Shuushuu-on
Shoo'oo-shoo'oo-ohn

123. Shinguru Torakku
Sheen-goo-roo Toh-rahk-koo

124. Shinguru Shisutemu
Sheen-goo-roo Shee-soo-teh-moo

125. Nameraka
Nah-meh-rah-kah

126. Yawarakai
Yah-wah-rah-kye

127. Soriddo Suteeto
Soh-reed-doh Soo-teh'eh-toh

128. Sound:

  a.   -edit

  b.   -effect

  c.   -head

  d.   -proof

  e.   -library

  f.   -recording

  g.   report

  h.   tape

129. Sound-on-film

130. Speaker

131. Splice:

  a.   bevel

  b.   straight

  c.   taped

128. Onsei/Oto:
     Ohn-say/Oh-toh:

   a.   -henshuu
        -hen-shoo'oo

   b.   -kooka
        -koh'oh-kah

   c.   -heddo
        -hehd-doh

   d.   -boo-on
        -boh'oh-ohn

   e.   saundo raiburari
        s'ow'n-doh rye-boo-rah-ree

   f.   -rokuon
        -roh-koo-ohn

   g.   rokuon jootai chekku
        roh-koo-ohn joh'oh-tye chehk-koo

   h.   -rokuon teepu
        -roh-koo-ohn teh'eh-poo

129. Fuirumu ni Rokuon Sareta Oto
     Foo-ee-roo-mah nee Roh-koo-ohn Sah-reh-
                              tah Oh-toh

130. Supiikaa
     Soo-pee'ee-kah'ah

131. Supuraisu:
     Soo-poo-rye-soo:

   a.   naname-
        nah-nah-meh-

   b.   chokusen-
        choh-koo-sehn-

   c.   teepu shiyoo-
        teh'eh-poo shee-yoh'oh-

132. Static

133. Stereophonic

134. Switch

135. Sync

136. Synchronous

137. Sync Mark

138. Sync Pops

139. Sync Pulse

140. Take

141. Talk-back

142. Tape Recorder

143. Toggle-switch

144. Tone

145. Track

146. Transcribe

132. Seidenki
Say-dehn-kee

133. Sutereo
Soo-teh-reh-oh

134. Suicchi
Soo-eet-chee

135. Doochoo
Doh'oh-choh'oh

136. Shinkuronasu
Sheen-koo-roh-nah-soo

137. Shinku Maaku
Sheen-koo Mah'ah-koo

138. Doochoo Yoo Aizu-on
Doh'oh-choh'oh Yoh'oh Eye-zoo-ohn

139. Shinku Parasu
Sheen-koo Pah-rah-soo

140. Saiyoo
Sye-yoh'oh

141. Kaiwa Soochi
Kye-wah Soh'oh-chee

142. Teepu Rekoodaa
Teh'eh-poo Reh-koh'oh-dah'ah

143. Toguru Suicchi
Toh-goo-roo Soo-eet-chee

144. Onchoo
Ohn-choh'oh

145. Torakku
Toh-rahk-koo

146. Rokuon Hoosoo
Roh-koo-ohn Hoh'oh-soh'oh

147. Transfer

148. Transistor

149. Tube

150. Turntable

151. Treble

152. Upper Register

153. Virgin Tape

154. Voice Level

155. VU (Volume Units) Meter

156. Meter

157. Wow

Useful Terms:

158. Composite Track (voice, music, effects)

159. Dialogue Track

160. Do Not Magnetize

147. Tensoo
     Tehn-soh'oh

148. Toranjisutaa
     Toh-rahn-jee-soo-tah'ah

149. Chuubu
     Choo'oo-boo

150. Taan Teeburu
     Tah'ahn Teh'eh-boo-roo

151. Koo-on/Toreburu
     Koh'oh-ohn/Toh-reh-boo-roo

152. Koo-oniki
     Koh'oh-oh-nee-kee

153. Mishiyoo Teepu
     Mee-shee-yoh'oh Teh'eh-poo

154. Boisu Reberu
     Boy-soo Reh-beh-roo

155. Boryuumukei
     Boh-r'yoo'oo-moo-kay

156. Keiki
     Kay-kee

157. Kaiten Mura
     Kye-tehn Moo-rah

Yakunitatsu Kotoba:
Yahk-nee-tah-tsoo Koh-toh-bah:

158. Goosei Torakku (Boisu,Ongaku,Kooka)
     Goh'oh-say Toh-rahk-koo (Boy-soo, Ohn-
     gah-koo, Koh'oh-kah)

159. Kaiwa Torakku
     Kye-wah Toh-rahk-koo

160. Jiki o Chikazukeruna
     Jee-kee o Chee-kah-zoo-keh-roo-nah

Useful Terms (continued):

161. Effects Track

162. Master

163. Music and Effects Combined

164. Music Track

165. To Be Transfered

166. Voice Track

Yakunitatsu Kotoba:
Yahk-nee-tah-tsoo Koh-toh-bah:

161. Kooka Torakku
     Koh'oh-kah Toh-rahk-koo

162. Masuta
     Mah-soo-tah

163. Ongaku Kooka Goosei
     Ohn-gah-koo Koh'oh-kah Goh'oh'say

164. Ongaku Torakku
     Ohn-gah-koo Toh-rahk-koo

165. Tensha Sareru
     Tehn-shah Sah-reh-roo

166. Onsei Torakku
     Ohn-say Toh-rahk-koo

01. Above The Line

02. Accounting

03. Advertising

04. Agent

05. Agreement

06. Audit

07. Authority

08. Below The Line

09. Bookkeeping

10. Budget:

  a.   final

  b.   over-

  c.   preliminary

  d.   under-

  e   within

SAY-SAH-KOO JEE-MOO YOH'OH-GOH

01. Hyoojun Ijoo
    H'yoh'oh-joon Ee-joh'oh

02. Keiri
    Kay-ree

03. Kookoku
    Koh'oh-koh-koo

04. Dairiten
    Dye-ree-tehn

05. Gooi
    Goh-oy

06. Kansa
    Kahn-sah

07. Tookyoku
    Toh'oh-k'oh-koo

08. Suijun Ika
    Soo-ee-joon Ee-kah

09. Boki
    Boh-kee

10. Yosan:
    Yoh-sahn:

  a. saishuu
      sye-shoo'oo

  b. -kajoo
      -kah-joh'oh

  c. toosho
      toh'oh-shoh

  d. -ika
      -ee-kah

  e. -nai
      -nye

11. Business

12. Buyout

13. Clearance

14. Completion Bond

15. Confirmation

16. Contract

17. Corporate Overhead Expense

18. Corporation

19. Department Head

20. Disbursements

21. Distribution

22. Employ

23. Employer

24. Entertainment

25. Executive

11. **Jigyoo**
   Jee-g'yoh'oh

12. **Baishuu**
   Bye-shoo'oo

13. **Tetsuzuki**
   Teh-tsoo-zoo-kee

14. **Ukeoi Keiyaku**
   Oo-keh-oy Kay-yah-koo

15. **Kakunin**
   Kah-koo-neen

16. **Keiyaku**
   Kay-yah-koo

17. **Hitori Atarino Hiyoo**
   Hee-toh-ree Ah-tah-ree-noh Hee-yoh'oh

18. **Kaisha**
   Kye-shah

19. **Bumon-choo**
   Boo-mohn-choh'oh

20. **Shiharai**
   Shee-hah-rye

21. **Bunpai**
   Boon-pye

22. **Koyoo**
   Koh-yoh'oh

23. **Koyoosha**
   Koh-yoh'oh-shah

24. **Settai**
   Seht-tye

25. **Keieisha**
   Kay-ay-shah

26. Exhibition

27. Fee

28. Finance

29. Financing

30. General Office Overhead

31. Incorporate

32. Independent Contractor

33. Insurance:

   a.   life

   b.   public liability

   c.   disability

   d.   worker's compensation

   e.   accident

34. Joint Venture

35. Investor

26. Tenji
    Tehn-jee

27. Hiyoo
    Hee-yoh'oh

28. Zaimu
    Zye-moo

29. Shikin Chootatsu
    Shee-keen Choh'oh-tah-tsoo

30. Hitori Atarino Jimusho Hiyoo
    *Hee-toh-ree Ah-tah-ree-noh Jee-moo-shoh
    Hee-yoh'oh*

31. Setsuritsu
    Seht-soo-ree-tsoo

32. Dokuritsu Keiyakusha
    Doh-koo-ree-tsoo Kay-yah-koo-shah

33. Hoken:
    Hoh-kehn:

  a.   seimei
       say-may

  b.   sekinin
       seh-kee-neen

  c.   fugu
       foo-goo

  d.   shitsugyoo
       shee-tsoo-g'yoh'oh

  e.   jiko
       jee-koh

34. Gooben Jigyoo
    Goh'oh-behn Jee-g'yoh'oh

35. Tooshika
    Toh'oh-shee-kah

36. Lease

37. Legal Counsel

38. Legal Fees

39. License

40. Limited Partners

41. Location Scouting

42. Management

43. Miscellaneous

44. Money

45. Negotiation

46. Office

47. Officer:

a.   President

b.   Executive Vice-President

c.   Vice-President

36. Riisu
    Ree'ee-soo

37. Hooritsu Soodan
    Hoh'oh-ree-tsoo Soh'oh-dahn

38. Hooritsu Hiyoo
    Hoh'oh-ree-tsoo Hee-yoh'oh

39. Menkyo
    Mehn-k'yoh

40. Yuugen Sekininsha
    Yoo'oo-gehn Seh-kee-neen-shah

41. Basho Sentai
    Bah-shoh Sehn-tye

42. Keiei
    Kay-ay

43. Zatsu/Sonota
    Zaht-soo/Soh-noh-tah

44. Kane/Kinsen
    Kah-neh/Keen-sehn

45. Kooshoo
    Koh'oh-shoh'oh

46. Jimusho
    Jee-moo-shoh

47. Yakushokusha:
    Yah-koo-shoh-koo-shah:

  a.   shachoo
       shah-choh'oh

  b.   jookyuu fukushachoo
       joh'oh-k'yoo'oo foo-koo-shah-choh'oh

  c.   fukushachoo
       foo-koo-shah-choh'oh

47. Officer (continued)

   d.   Treasurer

   e.   Secretary

   f.   Chairperson

   g.   Chairperson of the Board

   h.   Chief Executive Officer

48. Outside Expenses

49. Partnership

50. Pension Contributions

51. Permission

52. Permit

53. Phone and Telegraph

54. Policy

55. Preview

47. Yakushokusah (tsuzuku):
    Yah-koo-shoh-koo-shah (tsoo-zoo-koo):

  d.   kaikei buchoo
        kye-kay boo-choh'oh

  e.   hisho
        hee-shoh

  f.   kaichoo
        kye-choh'oh

  g.   torishimariyaku kaichoo
        toh-ree-shee-mah-ree-yah-koo kye-choh'oh

  h.   daihyoo torishimariyaku
        dye-h'yoh'oh toh-ree-shee-mah-ree-yah-koo

48. Gaibu Hiyoo
    Gye-boo Hee-yoh'oh

49. Kyoodoo Keiei
    K'yoh'oh-doh'oh Kay-ay

50. Yooroo Nenkin
    Yoh'oh-roh'oh Nehn-keen

51. Kyoka
    K'yoh-kah

52. Kyokasho
    K'yoh-kah-shoh

53. Denwa Denpoo
    Den-wah Den-poh'oh

54. Hooshin
    Hoh'oh-sheen

55. Yokoku
    Yoh-koh-koo

56. Production:

  a.   pre-

  b.   post-

  c.   staff

57. Proprietor

58. Publicity

59. Purchases

60. Release

61. Rent and Utilities

62. Rentals

63. Rules

64. Salaries

65. Schedule

66. Staff

67. Star

56. Prodakushon:
    Proh-dah-koo-shohn:

  a.   puri-
     poo-ree-

  b.   posuto-
     poh-soo-toh-

  c.   -sutaffu
     -soo-tahf-foo

57. Shoyuusha
    Shoh-yoo'oo-shah

58. Paburishiti
    Pah-boo-ree-shee-tee

59. Koobai
    Koh'oh-bye

60. Happyoo
    Hahp-p'yoh'oh

61. Yachin Koonetsuhi
    Yah-cheen Koh'oh-neh-tsoo-hee

62. Rentaru Hiyoo
    Rehn-tah-roo Hee-yoh'oh

63. Kitei
    Kee-tay

64. Kyuuyo
    K'yoo'oo-yoh

65. Yotei
    Yoh-tay

66. Sutaffu
    Soo-tahf-foo

67. Sutaa
    Soo-tah'ah

68. Studio

69. Supplies and Postage

70. Taxes:

a.   business

b.   city

c.   corporate

d.   county

e.   federal

f.   municipal

g.   state

71. Travel Expense:

a.   airplane/automobile

b.   ship/train

c.   economy

d.   first class

68. Sutajio
    S'tah-jee-oh

69. Zappi Tsuushinhi
    Zah-pee Tsoo'oo-sheen-hee

70. Zeikin:
    Zay-keen:

   a.   jigyoozei
        jee-g'yoh'oh-zay

   b.   shizei
        shee-zay

   c.   hoojinzei
        hoh'oh-jeen-zay

   d.   gunzei
        goon-zay

   e.   renpoozei
        rehn-poh'oh-zay

   f.   shizei
        shee-zay

   g.   shuuzei
        shoo'oo-zay

71. Ryohi:
    R'yoh-hee:

   a.   hikooki/jidoosha
        hee-koh'oh-kee/jee-doh'oh-shah

   b.   fune/kisha
        foo-neh/kee-shah

   c.   ekonomii
        eh-koh-noh-mee'ee

   d.   itto/faasuto kurasu
        eet-toh/fah'ah-s'toh koo-rah-soo

Useful Terms:

72. Accounts Payable/Receivable

73. Charge To:

74. Credit/Debit

75. Hold In Suspense

76. Memo To:

77. Paid In Full

78. Verified

Yakunitatsu Kotoba:
Yahk-nee-tah-tsoo Koh-toh-bah:

72. **Kaikake/Urikake**
    Kye-kah-keh/Oo-ree-kah-keh

73. **Seikyuusaki**
    Say-k'yoo'oo-sah-kee

74. **Kashikata/Karikata**
    Kah-shee-kah-tah/Kah-ree-kah-tah

75. **Ichiji Horyuu**
    Ee-chee-jee Hoh-r'yoo'oo

76. **--Ate Memo**
    --Ah-teh Meh-moh

77. **Zengaku Shiharai**
    Zen-gah-koo Shee-hah-rye

78. **Kakujitsuna**
    Kah-koo-jee-tsoo-nah

01. Action

02. Add

03. Aside

04. Asterisk

05. Atmosphere

06. Audio

07. Away

08. Background (b.g.)

09. Caption

10. Character

11. Close (shut)

12. Continued

13. Cut

14. Dash (—)

15. Day

01. Akushon
    Ah-koo-shohn

02. Tsuika
    Tsoo-ee-kah

03. Yoko Ni
    Yoh-koh Nee

04. Hoshi Jirushi
    Hoh-shee Jee-roo-shee

05. Funiki
    Foon-ee-kee

06. Oto
    Oh-toh

07. Tooku
    Toh'oh-koo

08. Haikei
    Hye-kay

09. Kyapushon
    K'yahp-shohn

10. Jinbutsu
    Jeen-boo-tsoo

11. Tojiru
    Toh-jee-roo

12. Tsuzuku
    Tsoo-zoo-koo

13. Katto
    Kaht-toh

14. Dasshu
    Dahs-shoo

15. Hi
    Hee

16. Delete

17. Dialect

18. Dialogue

19. Dissolve

20. Down

21. Downstage

22. Effect

23. Enter

24. Eraser

25. Exclamation Point

26. Exit

27. Exterior

28. Fade-in

29. Fade-out

30. Footnote

16. Kesu
    Keh-soo

17. Hoogen
    Hoh'oh-gehn

18. Kaiwa/Daiarogu
    Kye-wah/Dye-ah-roh-goo

19. Bokasu
    Boh-kah-soo

20. Shitae
    Shee-tah-eh

21. Butai
    Boo-tye

22. Kooka
    Koh'oh-kah

23. Iriguchi
    Ee-ree-goo-chee

24. Keshigomu
    Keh-shee-goh-moo

25. Kantanfu
    Kahn-tahn-foo

26. Deguchi
    Deh-goo-chee

27. Gaibu
    Gye-boo

28. Feido-in
    Fay-doh-een

29. Feido-auto
    Fay-doh-ow-toh

30. Kyakuchuu
    K'yah-koo-choo'oo

31. From

32. Glossary

33. Hyphen

34. Indent

35. Index

36. In Frame

37. Ink

38. Intercut

39. Interior

40. Interpret

41. Language

42. Left

43. Left-to-right

44. Mood

45. More

31. --Kara
    --Kah-rah

32. Yoogoshuu
    Yoh'oh-goh-shoo'oo

33. Haifun
    Hye-foon

34. Gyoosage
    G'yoh'oh-sah-geh

35. Sakuin
    Sah-koo-een

36. Fureemu Nai
    Foo-reh'eh-moo Nye

37. Inku
    Een-koo

38. Tochuu Soonyuu
    Toh-choo'oo Soh'oh-n'yoo'oo

39. Interia
    Een-teh-ree-ah

40. Honyaku
    Hohn-yah-koo

41. Gengo
    Gehn-goh

42. Hidari
    Hee-dah-ree

43. Hidari Kara Migi E
    Hee-dah-ree Kah-rah Mee-gee Eh

44. Muudo
    Moo'oo-doh

45. Motto
    Moh-toh

46. Narration

47. Night

48. Notation

49. Off-screen (o.s.)

50. Open

51. Out-of-frame

52. Page

53. Pen

54. Pencil

55. Period (.)

56. Picture

57. Plot

58. Point Of View (P.O.V.)

59. Question Mark

60. Quote

46. Nareeshon
    Nah-reh'eh-shohn

47. Yoru
    Yoh-roo

48. Chuushaku
    Choo'oo-shah-koo

49. Sukuriin Gai
    Soo-koo-ree'een Gye

50. Hiraku
    Hee-rah-koo

51. Fureemu Gai
    Foo-reh'eh-moo Gye

52. Peeji/Yobidashi
    Peh'eh-jee/Yoh-bee-dah-shee

53. Pen
    Pehn

54. Enpitsu
    Ehn-pee-tsoo

55. Piriodo
    Pee-ree-oh-doh

56. Shashin
    Shah-sheen

57. Koosoo
    Koh'oh-soh'oh

58. Shiten
    Shee-tehn

59. Gimonfu
    Gee-mohn-foo

60. Inyoo
    Een-yoh'oh

61. Re-write

62. Right

63. Right-to-left

64. Ruler (measuring)

65. Scenario

66. Scene

67. Screenplay

68. Script

69. Sequence

70. Shooting Script

71. Shot

72. Sound

73. Stage Left

74. Stage Right

75. Story

61. Kakinaoshi
Kah-kee-nah-oh-shee

62. Migi
Mee-gee

63. Migi Kara Hidari E
Mee-gee Kah-rah Hee-dah-ree Eh

64. Monosashi
Moh-noh-sah-shee

65. Daihon/Shinario
Dye-hohn/Shee-nah-ree-oh

66. Shiin
Shee'een

67. Daihon
Dye-hohn

68. Genkoo
Gehn-koh'oh

69. Renzoku
Rehn-zoh-koo

70. Kamerayoo Daihon
Kah-meh-rah-yoh'oh Dye-hohn

71. Bamen
Bah-mehn

72. Oto
Oh-toh

73. Butai Hidari E
Boo-tye Hee-dah-ree Eh

74. Butai Migi E
Boo-tye Mee-gee Eh

75. Sutoorii/Suji
Soo-toh'oh-ree'ee/Soo-jee

76. Synopsis

77. Sub-plot

78. Superimpose

79. The End

80. Theme

81. Title

82. To

83. Toward

84. Treatment

85. Type

86. Typewriter

87. Typewriter Ribbon

88. Write

89. Video

76. Gairyaku
    Gye-r'yah-koo

77. Hojoteki Koosoo
    Hoh-joh-teh-kee Koh'oh-soh'oh

78. Suupaainpoozu
    Soo'oo-pah'ah-een-poh'oh-zoo

79. Owari
    Oh-wah-ree

80. Teema
    Teh'eh-mah

81. Taitoru
    Tye-toh-roo

82. --E
    --Eh

83. --E
    --Eh

84. Toriatsukai
    Toh-ree-aht-soo-kye

85. Taipusuru Katsuji
    Tye-poo-soo-roo Kah-tsoo-jee

86. Taipuraitaa
    Tye-poo-rye-tah'ah

87. Taipuyoo Ribon
    Tye-poo-yoh'oh Ree-bohn

88. Kaku
    Kah-koo

89. Bideo
    Bee-deh-oh

<u>Useful Terms</u>:

90. First Draft

91. Final

92. Revised

93. Approved

94. Registered

95. Copyright

96. Original Script

97. O.K. To Duplicate

98. Send To Printer

Yakunitatsu Kotoba:
Yahk-nee-tah-tsoo Koh-toh-bah:

90. Saisho No Genkoo
    Sye-shoh Noh Gehn-koh'oh

91. Saishuu
    Sye-shoo'oo

92. Henkoosareta
    Hehn-koh'oh-sah-reh-tah

93. Shooninsareta
    Shoh'oh-een-sah-reh-tah

94. Toorokusareta
    Toh'oh-roh-koo-sah-reh-tah

95. Chosakuken
    Choh-sah-koo-ken

96. Moton Genkoo
    Moh-tohn Gehn-koh'oh

97. Kopiishite Yoi
    Koh-pee'ee-shee-teh Yoy

98. Purinto E Okure
    Poo-reen-toh Eh Oh-koo-reh

01. Awl

02. Belt

03. Blade

04. Block-and-tackle

05. Blowtorch

06. Bolt

07. Broom

08. Brush:

  a.   artist's

  b.   camel's-hair

  c.   paint

  d.   wire

  e.   narrow

  f.   wide

09. Bull-horn

Koh'oh-goo

01. **Kiri**
Kee-ree

02. **Beruto**
Beh-roo-toh

03. **Ha**
Hah

04. **Chieen Burokku**
Chee-eh'ehn Boo-rohk-koo

05. **Haikanyoo Toochi**
Hye-kahn-yoh'oh Toh'oh-chee

06. **Boruto**
Boh-roo-toh

07. **Hooki**
Hoh'oh-kee

08. **Burashi/Hake:**
Boo-rah-shee/Hah-keh:

  a.   **kaigayoo**
     kye-gah-yoh'oh

  b.   **rakudage**
     rah-koo-dah-geh

  c.   **penkiyoo**
     pehn-kee-yoh'oh

  d.   **waiyaa**
     wye-yah

  e.   **haba no semai-**
     hah-bah noh seh-mye-

  f.   **haba no hiroi**
     hah-bah noh hee-roy

09.   **Ushi no Tsuno**
    Oo-shee no Tsoo-noh

10. Caliper

11. C-clamp

12. Chisel:

 a. metal

 b. narrow-blade

 c. wide-blade

 d. wood

13. Compass

14. Countersink

15. Dividers

16. Drill:

 a. concrete

 b. metal-cutting

 c. "star"

 d. wood-cutting

10. Nogisu
    Noh-gee-soo

11. Kuranpu
    Koo-rahn-poo

12. Nomi:
    Noh-mee:

   a.   kinzokuyoo
      Keen-zoh-koo-yoh'oh

   b.   haba no semai-
      Hah-bah noh seh-mye-

   c.   haba no hiroi-
      hah-bah noh hee-roy-

   d.   mokkooyoo
      mohk-koh'oh-yoh'oh

13. Konpasu
    Kohn-pah-soo

14. Saramomi
    Sah-rah-moh-mee

15. Debaidaa/Shiriki
    Deh-bye-dah'ah/Shee-ree-kee

16. Doriru:
    Doh-ree-roo:

   a.   konkuriitoyoo
      kohn-koo-ree'ee-toh-yoh'oh

   b.   kinzokuyoo
      keen-zoh-koo-yoh'oh

   c.   hoshigata
      hoh-shee-gah-tah

   d.   mokkooyoo
      mohk-koh'oh-yoh'oh

17. English Scale

18. File:

a.   bastard

b.   half-round

c.   mill

d.   pointed

e.   round

f.   tapered

19. Flaring Tool

20. Flashlight

21. Fuse Puller

22. Gloves

23. Hammer:

a.   ball pein

b.   claw

17. Igirisu-shiki
    Ee-gee-ree-soo-shee-kee

18. Yasuri:
    Yah-soo-ree:

 a.   arame
      ah-rah-meh

 b.   hanmarui
      hahn-mah-roo-ee

 c.   shiage
      shee-ah-geh

 d.   sakiboso
      sah-kee-boh-so

 e.   marui
      mah-roo-ee

 f.   teipu no tsuita
      tay-poo noh tsoo-ee-tah

19. Paipu Kaikoobu Kakudaiyoo Koogu
    Pye-poo Kye-koh'oh-boo Kah-koo-dye-yoh'oh
    Koh'oh-goo

20. Furasshu Raito
    Foo-rahs-shoo Rye-toh

21. Hyuuzu Nuki
    H'yoo'oo-zoo Noo-kee

22. Tebukuro
    Teh-boo-koo-roh

23. Hanmaa:
    Hahn-mah'ah:

 a.   maru atama tsuki
      mah-roo ah-tah-mah tsoo-kee

 b.   kuginuki tsuki
      koo-gee-noo-kee tsoo-kee

23. Hammer (continued):

c.   machinest's

d.   rawhide

e.   rubber

f.   scaling

g.   sledge

h.   tack

i.   upholsterer's

24. Handle

25. Hoe

26. Hoist

27. Hook

28. Jack:

a.   hydraulic

b.   screw

23. Hanmaa (tsuzuku):
    Hahn-mah'ah (tsoo-zoo-koo):

  c. kikaikoo
     kee-kye-koh'oh

  d. kawa de maita
     kah-wah deh mye-tah

  e. gomu sei
     goh-moo say

  f. nomi no yoona
     noh-mee noh yoh'oh-nah

  g. ookii
     oh'oh-kee'ee

  h. byoo uchi yoo
     b'yoh'oh oo-chee yoh'oh

  i. kagu yoo
     kah-goo yoh'oh

24. Handoru
    Hahn-doh-roo

25. Kuwa
    Koo-wah

26. Hoisuto
    Hoy-soo-toh

27. Fukku
    Fook-koo

28. Jakki:
    Jahk-kee:

  a. yuatsu shiki
     yoo-ah-tsoo shee-kee

  b. neji shiki
     neh-jee shee-kee

29. Kit

30. Knife:

a.   carpet

b.   electrician's

c.   hunting

d.   pocket

e.   putty

f.   razor-blade

31. Lubricant:

a.   grease

b.   grease-gun

c.   oil

d.   oil can

e.   oil spout

f.   rustproof

29. Kitto
    Keet-toh

30. Naifu:
    Nye-foo:

 a.   kaapetto yoo
      kah'ah-peht-toh yoh'oh

 b.   denkikoo yoo
      den-kee-koh'oh yoh'oh

 c.   shuryoo yoo
      shoo-r'yoh'oh yoh'oh

 d.   poketto
      poh-keht-toh

 e.   pate
      pah-teh

 f.   kamisori no ha
      kah-mee-soh-ree noh hah

31. Junkatsu zai:
    Joon-kah-tsoo zye:

 a.   guriisu
      goo-ree'ee-soo

 b.   guriisu chuunyuu yoogu
      goo-ree'ee-soo choo'oon-yoo'oo yoh'oh-goo

 c.   abura
      ah-boo-rah

 d.   sekiyu kan
      seh-kee-yoo kahn

 e.   abura sashi
      ah-boo-rah sah-shee

 f.   boosei
      boh'oh-say

32. Magnifying Glass

33. Measuring Tape:

a.   carpenter's

b.   cloth

c.   folding

d.   metal

e.   pocket

f.   ruler

34. Metric Scale

35. Nail

36. Needle:

a.   hypodermic

b.   sailmaker's

c.   sewing

d.   tailor's

32. Kakudaikyoo
    Kah-koo-dye-k'yoh'oh

33. Makijaku:
    Mah-kee-jah-koo:

   a. daiku yoo
       dye-koo yoh'oh

   b. nuno sei
       noo-noh say

   c. orijaku
       oh-ree-jah-koo

   d. kinzoku sei
       keen-zoh-koo say

   e. poketto gata
       poh-keht-toh gah-tah

   f. monosashi
       moh-noh-sah-shee

34. Meetoru Hoo Monosashi
    Meh'eh-toh-roo Hoh'oh Moh-noh-sah-shee

35. Kugi
    Koo-gee

36. Hari:
    Hah-ree:

   a. chuusha yoo
       choo'oo-shah yoh'oh

   b. seiru yoo
       say-roo yoh'oh

   c. nuibari
       noo-ee-bah-ree

   d. shitate yoo
       shee-tah-teh yoh'oh

37. Nut

38. Pick

39. Pitchfork

40. Pliers:

 a.   battery

 b.   diagonals

 c.   fence

 d.   ignition

 e.   insulated-handle

 f.   knurled-handled

 g.   lineman's

 h.   needle-nose

 i.   serrated-jaw

 j.   side-cutting

 k.   slip-joint

37. Natto
    Naht-toh

38. Pikku
    Peek-koo

39. Hooku
    Hoh'oh-koo

40. Puraiyaa:
    Poo-rye-yah'ah:

 a.   denchi yoo
      den-chee yoh'oh

 b.   taikakusen gata
      tye-kah-koo-sehn gah-tah

 c.   fensu yoo
      fehn-soo yoh'oh

 d.   puragu yoo
      poo-rah-goo yoh'oh

 e.   zetsuen shiki
      zeht-soo-ehn shee-kee

 f.   suberidome tsuki
      soo-beh-ree-doh-meh tsoo-kee

 g.   denkikoo yoo
      den-kee-koh'oh yoh'oh

 h.   yattoko
      yaht-toh-koh

 i.   nokogirijoo
      noh-koh-gee-ree-joh'oh

 j.   penchi
      pehn-chee

 k.   puraiyaa
      poo-rye-yah'ah

40. Pliers (continued):

   l.   smooth-jaw

   m.   snap-ring

   n.   water pump

   o.   wire-cutting

41. Pouch

42. Pry Bar

43. Punch

44. Rake

45. Rivet

46. Rivet Gun

47. Safety Goggles

48. Saw:

   a.   back-

   b.   electrical-powered

40. Puraiyaa (tsuzuku):
    Poo-rye-yah'ah (tsoo-zoo-koo):

  l. arumi kuchi tsuki
      ah-roo-mee koo-chee tsoo-kee

  m. kintei wasshaa yoo
      keen-tay wahs-shah'ah yoh'oh

  n. ponpu yoo
      pohn-poo yoh'oh

  o. waiyaa kiri
      wye-yah'ah kee-ree

41. Kobukuro
    Koh-boo-koo-roh

42. Baaru
    Bah'ah-roo

43. Panchi
    Pahn-chee

44. Kumade
    Koo-mah-deh

45. Ribetto
    Ree-beht-toh

46. Ribetto Gan
    Ree-beht-toh Gahn

47. Anzen Megane
    Ahn-zen Meh-gah-neh

48. Nokogiri:
    Noh-koh-gee-ree:

  a. seiyoo
      say-yoh'oh

  b. dendoo
      den-doh'oh

48. Saw (continued):

c.   hack-

d.   hand-

e.   keyhole

f.   metal

g.   tree-

49. Scraper

50. Screw

51. Screwdriver:

a.   insulated

b.   jeweler's

c.   large

d.   medium

e.   offset

f.   Phillips

48. Nokogiri (tsuzuku):
    Noh-koh-gee-ree (tsoo-zoo-koo):

  c. kinzoku
     keen-zoh-koo

  d. temochi
     teh-moh-chee

  e. itonoko
     ee-toh-noh-koh

  f. kinzoku
     keen-zoh-koo

  g. mokkoo yoo
     mohk-koh'oh yoh'oh

49. Hera
    Heh-rah

50. Neji
    Neh-jee

51. Doraibaa:
    Doh-rye-bah'ah:

  a. zetsuen
     zeht-soo-ehn

  b. hooseki yoo
     hoh'oh-seh-kee yoh'oh

  c. oogata
     oh'oh-gah-tah

  d. chuugata
     choo'oo-gah-tah

  e. ofusetto
     ohf-seht-toh

  f. purasu
     poo-rah-soo

51. Screwdriver (continued):

  g.   plastic

  h.   small

  i.   straight-blade

  j..   technician's

52. Shank

53. Sheave

54. Shovel

55. Solder

56. Soldering Iron

57. Spade

58. Sponge

59. Swivel

60. Stopwatch

51. Doraibaa (tsuzuku):
    Doh-rye-bah'ah (tsoo-zoo-koo):

  g.   purasuchikku
       poo-rah-soo-cheek-koo

  h.   kogata
       koh-gah-tah

  i.   mainasu
       mye-nah-soo

  j.   tekunishan yoo
       teh-koo-nee-shahn yoh'oh

52. Nigiri
    Nee-gee-ree

53. Kassha
    Kahs-shah

54. Shaberu
    Shah-beh-roo

55. Handa Zuke
    Hahn-dah Zoo-keh

56. Handa Gote
    Hahn-dah Goh-teh

57. Shaberu
    Shah-beh-roo

58. Suponji
    Soo-pohn-jee

59. Sarukan
    Sah-roo-kahn

60. Sutoppu Uocchi
    Soo-tohp-poo Oo-oht-chee

61. Tape:

a. black

b. camera

c. cloth

d. double-face

e. electrician's

f. gaffer's

g. masking

h. paper

62. Tin Snips

63. Tool Box

64. Trowel:

a. brick

b. jointer

c. linoleum

61. Teepu:
    Teh'eh-poo:

 a.   kuroi
    koo-roy

 b.   kamero yoo
    kah-meh-roh yoh'oh

 c.   nuno sei
    noo-noh say

 d.   ryoomen
    r'yoh'oh-mehn

 e.   denkikoo yoo
    den-kee-koh'oh yoh'oh

 f.   denki yoo
    den-kee yoh'oh

 g.   masuku
    mah-soo-koo

 h.   kami sei
    kah-mee say

62. Buriki Hasami
    Boo-ree-kee Hah-sah-mee

63. Koogu Bako
    Koh'oh-goo Bah-koh

64. Kote:
    Koh-teh:

 a.   renga yoo
    rehn-gah yoh'oh

 b.   shiage yoo
    shee-ah-geh yoh'oh

 c.   rinoryuumu yoo
    ree-noh-r'yoo'oo-moo yoh'oh

64. Trowel (continued):

  d.   planting

  e.   plastering

  f.   pointing

65. Tube Cutter

66. Welding Torch

67. Winch

68. Wire Stripper

69. Work Light

70. Wrench:

  a.   adjustable

  b.   close-ended

  c.   combination

  d.   mechanic's

  e.   open-ended

64. Kote (tsuzuku):
    Koh-teh (tsoo-zoo-koo):

 d.   engei yoo
      ehn-gay yoh'oh

 e.   sakan yoo
      sah-kahn yoh'oh

 f.   saki no togatta
      sah-kee noh toh-gaht-tah

65. Chuubu Kiri
    Choo'oo-boo Kee-ree

66. Yoosetsuki
    Yoh'oh-seh-tsoo-kee

67. Uinchi
    Oo-een-chee

68. Hifuku Hagashi
    Hee-foo-koo Hah-gah-shee

69. Sagyoo Yoo Dentoo
    Sah-g'yoh'oh Yoh'oh Den-toh'oh

70. Renchi:
    Rehn-chee:

 a.   choosetsu
      choh'oh-seh-tsoo

 b.   kuroozu endo
      koo-roh'oh-zoo ehn-doh

 c.   kumiawase shiki
      koo-mee-ah-wah-seh shee-kee

 d.   kikaikoo
      kee-kye-koh'oh

 e.   oopun endo
      oh'oh-poon ehn-doh

70. Wrench (continued):

f.   plumber's

g.   ratchet

h.   socket

i.   torque

Useful Terms:

71. Keep Out

72. Keep Off

73. Wet Paint

74. Hard Hat Required

75. Wear Safety Glasses

76. Unsafe

77. First Aid Kit

78. Fire Extinguisher

79. In An Emergency Call....

70. Renchi (tsuzuku):
    Rehn-chee (tsoo-zoo-koo):

  f.   haikankoo yoo
       hye-kahn-koh'oh yoh'oh

  g.   rachetto tsuki
       rah-cheht-toh tsoo-kee

  h.   soketto yoo
       soh-keht-toh yoh'oh

  i.   toruku
       toh-roo-koo

Yakunitatsu Kotoba:
Yahk-nee-tah-tsoo Koh-toh-bah:

71. Tachiiri Kinshi
    Tah-chee'ee-ree Keen-shee

72. Tachiiri Kinshi
    Tah-chee'ee-ree Keen-shee

73. Penki Nuritate
    Pehn-kee Noo-ree-tah-teh

74. Herumetto Chakuyoo
    Heh-roo-meht-toh Chah-koo-yoh'oh

75. Hogo Megane Chakuyoo
    Hoh-goh Meh-gah-neh Chah-koo-yoh'oh

76. Kiken
    Kee-kehn

77. Kyuukyuu Yoohin
    K'yoo'oo-k'yoo'oo Yoh'oh-heen

78. Shookaki
    Shoh'oh-kah-kee

79. Kin Kyuu Denwa ___ Shite Kudasai
    Keen K'yoo'oo Den-wah ___ Shee-teh Koo-dah-sye

01. Adjust

02. Ambience

03. Amplifier

04. Amplify

05. Amplitude

06. Anode

07. Antenna

08. Apparatus

09. Aspect Ratio

10. Audio

11. Automatic Gain Control

12. Beam-splitter

13. Bias

14. Black Level

15. Blanking

01. **Choosei**
Choh'oh-say

02. **Fuyoona Hikari**
Foo-yoh'oh-nah Hee-kah-ree

03. **Zoofukuki**
Zoh'oh-foo-koo-kee

04. **Zoofuku Suru**
Zoh'oh-foo-koo Soo-roo

05. **Shinpuku**
Sheen-poo-koo

06. **Anoodo/Yookyoku**
Ah-noh'oh-doh/Yoh'oh-k'yoh-koo

07. **Antena**
Ahn-teh-nah

08. **Soochi**
Soh'oh-chee

09. **Asupekuto**
Ah-soo-peh-koo-toh

10. **Oto**
Oh-toh

11. **Jidoo Gein Kontorooru**
Jee-doh'oh Gayn Kohn-toh-roh'oh-roo

12. **Biimu Supurittaa**
Bee'ee-moo S'p'reet-tah'ah

13. **Baiasu**
Bye-ah-soo

14. **Burakku Reberu**
Boo-rahk-koo Reh-beh-roo

15. **Burankingu**
Boo-rahn-keen-goo

16. Blanking Pulse

17. Bloom

18. Booster

19. Brightness

20. Calibrate

21. Cathode

22. Camera Chain

23. Channel

24. Chroma

25. Chroma-key

26. Chrominance

27. Circuit

28. Clip (cut-off)

29. Closed Circuit

30. Co-axial Cable

16. Burankingu Parusu
    B'rahn-keen-goo Pah-roo-soo

17. Shironuke
    Shee-roh-noo-keh

18. Buusutaa
    Boo'oo-s'tah'ah

19. Kido
    Kee-doh

20. Choosei Suru
    Choh'oh-say Soo-roo

21. Kasoodo/Inkyoku
    Kah-soh'oh-doh/Een-k'yoh-koo

22. Tereshine
    Teh-reh-shee-neh

23. Channeru
    Chahn-neh-roo

24. Saido
    Sye-doh

25. Kurooma Kii
    Koo-roh'oh-mah Kee'ee

26. Saido No Takai Iro
    Sye-doh Noh Tah-kye Ee-roh

27. Kairo
    Kye-roh

28. Kurippu
    Koo-reep-poo

29. Heikairo
    Hay-kye-roh

30. Doojiku Keeburu
    Doh'oh-jee-koo Keh'eh-boo-roo

31. Color:

a.   -balance

b.   -bars

c.   -killer

d.   temperature

32. Commercial

33. Compatible

34. Compositor

35. Confetti

36. Console

37. Contrast

38. Contrast Range

39. Control

40. Control Room

41. Convergence

31. Karaa/Iro:
    Kah-rah'ah/Ee-roh:

  a. -baransu
      -bah-rahn-soo

  b. -baa
      -bah'ah

  c. -kiraa
      -kee-rah'ah

  d. -ondo
      -ohn-doh

32. Komaasharu
    Koh-mah'ah-shah-roo

33. Ryooritsu Shiki
    R'yoh'oh-ree-tsoo Shee-kee

34. Konpojitaa
    Kohn-poh-jee-tah'ah

35. Shikishihen
    Shee-kee-shee-hen

36. Konsooru
    Kohn-soh'oh-roo

37. Kontorasuto
    Kohn-toh-rah-soo-toh

38. Kontorasuto Renji
    Kohn-toh-rah-soo-toh Rehn-jee

39. Choosei
    Choh'oh-say

40. Choosei Shitsu
    Choh'oh-say Shee-tsoo

41. Shuuren/Konbaajensu
    Shoo'oo-rehn/Kohn-bah'ah-jehn-soo

42. Copy

43. Cue

44. Current

45. Damping

46. DC Restorer

47. Definition

48. Deflecting Yoke

49. Detector

50. Diode

51. Distortion

52. Drop Frame

53. Duplicate

54. Duplicator

55. Edit

56 Electron Beam

42. Kopii
   Koh-pee'ee

43. Aizu
   Eye-zoo

44. Denryuu
   Den-r'yoo'oo

45. Kyuugeki
   K'yoo'oo-geh-kee

46. Dii Shii Kikan
   Dee'ee Shee'ee Kee-kahn

47. Senmeido
   Sehn-may-doh

48. Henkoo Koiru
   Hehn-koh'oh Koy-roo

49. Kenshutsuki
   Kehn-shoo-tsoo-kee

50. Daioodo
   Dye-oh'oh-doh

51. Disutooshon
   Dee-s'toh'oh-shohn

52. Komaochi
   Koh-mah-oh-chee

53. Dyupurikeito
   D'yoo-poo-ree-kay-toh

54. Dyupurikeito
   D'yoo-poo-ree-kay-toh

55. Henshoo
   Hehn-sho'oh

56. Denshi Biimu
   Den-shee Bee'ee-moo

57. Electron Gun

58. Electronic Camera

59. Exposure:

a.   over-

b.   under-

60. Field

61. Film-to-tape

62. Fine Tuning

63. Fringing

64. Gain

65. Gamma

66. Ghost

67. Grey Card

68. Grey Scale

69. Grid-leak

57. Denshi Juu
    Den-shee Joo'oo

58. Denshi Kamera
    Den-shee Kah-meh-rah

59. Roshutsu
    Roh-shoo-tsoo

  a.   -kata
       -kah-tah

  b.   -fusoku
       -foo-soh-koo

60. Fiirudo
    Fee'ee-roo-doh

61. Fuirumu Kara Teepu
    Foo-ee-roo-moo Kah-rah Teh'eh-poo

62. Bichoosei
    Bee-shoh'oh-say

63. Furinjingu
    Foo-reen-jeen-goo

64. Gein
    Gayn

65. Ganma
    Gahn-mah

66. Goosuto
    Goh'oh-soo-toh

67. Gurei Kaado
    Goo-ray Kah'ah-doh

68. Gurei Sukeeru
    Goo-ray S'keh'eh-roo

69. Guriddo Riiku
    Goo-reed-doh Ree'ee-koo

70. Headphones

71. High Band

72. Hold:

a.   horizontal

b.   vertical

73. Hue

74. Hum

75. Image

76. Image Plate

77. Impedence

78. In-frame Coding

79. Interference

80. Interlace

81. Joy-stick

82. Keystone

70. Heddohon
    Hehd-doh-hohn

71. Koo Bando
    Koh'oh Bahn-doh

72. Dooki:
    Doh'oh-kee:

   a.   suihei
         soo-ee-hay

   b.   suichoku
         soo-ee-choh-koo

73. Iroai
    Ee-roh-eye

74. Unarion
    Oo-nah-ree-ohn

75. Eizoo
    Ay-zoh'oh

76. Ketsuzoo Ban
    Keh-tsoo-zoh'oh Bahn

77. Inpidansu
    Een-pee-dahn-soo

78. Fureemu Wai Koodingu
    Foo-reh'eh-moo Wye Koh'oh-deen-goo

79. Kanshoo
    Kahn-shoh'oh

80. Intaareesu
    Een-tah'ah-reh'eh-soo

81. Soosa Kan
    Soh'oh-sah Kahn

82. Kiisutoon
    Kee'ee-s'toh'ohn

83. Kinescope

84. Knob

85. Line

86. Linear

87. Light-and-shade

88. Limiter

89. Luminance

90. Master

91. Matrix

92. Micro:

 a.   -switch

 b.   -volt

93. Modulation:

 a.   over-

 b.   under-

83. Kinesukoopu
   Kee-neh-soo-koh'oh-poo

84. Tsumami
   Tsoo-mah-mee

85. Rain
   Rye'n

86. Rinia
   Ree-nee-ah

87. Hikari To Kage
   Hee-kah-ree Toh Kah-geh

88. Rimittaa
   Ree-meet-tah'ah

89. Ruminansu
   Roo-mee-nahn-soo

90. Masutaa
   Mah-soo-tah'ah

91. Matorikusu
   Mah-toh-ree-koo-soo

92. Maikuro:
   Mye-koo-roh:

 a.   -suicchi
      -soo-eet-chee

 b.   -boruto
      -boh-roo-toh

93. Henchoo:
   Hehn-choo:

 a.   -kata
      -kah-tah

 b.   -fusoku
      -foo-soh-koo

94. Monitor

95. Multi-camera

96. Negative Image

97. Noise:

  a.   low-

  b.   high-

  c.   off-line

98. Oscilloscope

99. Peak

100. Pedestal

101. Phosphor

102. Photoconductor

103. Photoelectric Cell

104. Picture Tube

105. Pincushion Effect

94. Monitaa
    Moh-nee-tah'ah

95. Tasuu Kamera
    Tah-soo'oo Kah-meh-rah

96. Inga
    Een-gah

97. Noizu:
    Noy-zoo:

  a. tei-
      tay-

  b. koo-
      koh'oh-

  c. ofurain-
      oh-foo-rye'n-

98. Oshirosukoopu
    Oh-shee-roh-s'koh'oh-poo

99. Piiku
    Pee'ee-koo

100. Pedesutaru
     Peh-deh-s'tah-roo

101. Rinkoo
     Reen-koh'oh

102. Kooden Busshitsu
     Koh'oh-den Boos-sh'tsoo

103. Kooden Soochi
     Koh'oh-den Soh'oh-chee

104. Buraunkan
     Boo-r'ow'n-kahn

105. Itomaki Kooka
     Ee-toh-mah-kee Koh'oh-kah

106. Pipe Grid

107. Positive

108. Power Supply

109. Printed Circuit

110. Program

111. Pulse Shaper

112. Radiation

113. Range

114. Receiver

115. Raster

116. Red-Green-Blue (RGB)

117. Reflectance

118. Remote

119. Satellite

120. Saturation

106. Paipu Guriddo
Pye-poo Goo-reed-doh

107. Sei
Say

108. Dengen
Den-gehn

109. Purinto Ban
Poo-reen-toh Bahn

110. Puroguramu
Poo-roh-goo-rah-moo

111. Parusu Sheipaa
Pah-roo-soo Shay-pah'ah

112. Hoosha
Hoh'oh-shah

113. Renji
Rehn-jee

114. Reshiibaa
Reh-shee'ee-bah'ah

115. Rasutaa
Rah-soo-tah'ah

116. Aka Midori Ao
Ah-kah Mee-doh-ree Ah-oh

117. Rifurekutansu
Ree-foo-reh-koo-tahn-soo

118. Rimooto
Ree-moh'oh-toh

119. Eisei
Ay-say

120. Hoowa
Hoh'oh-wah

121. Sawtooth Waveform

122. Scanner

123. Secondary Emission

124. Selector Switch

125. Semi-conductor

126. Shunt

127. Signal

128. Signal-to-noise Ratio

129. Sine Wave

130. Slo-mo Disc

131. Snow

132. Straight Frame

133. Synchronizer

134. Switcher (vision mixer panel)

135. Sync Generator

121. Nokogiri Ha
Noh-koh-gee-ree Hah

122. Sukyanaa
S'k'yah-nah'ah

123. Niji Hoosha
Nee-jee Hoh'oh-shah

124. Sentaku Suicchi
Sehn-tah-koo Soo-eet-chee

125. Handootai
Hahn-doh'oh-tye

126. Bunro
Boon-roh

127. Shingoo
Sheen-goh'oh

128. Esu Enu Hi
Eh-soo Eh-noo Hee

129. Sain Kaabu
Syne Kah'ah-boo

130. Suroo Mooshon Disuku
Soo-roh'oh Moh'oh-shohn Dee-s'koo

131. Sunoo
Soo-noh'oh

132. Chokusen Fureemu
Choh-koo-sehn Foo-reh'eh-moo

133. Shinkuronaizaa
Sheen-k'roh-nye-zah'ah

134. Suicchaa
Soo-eet-chah'ah

135. Shinku Jenereetaa
Sheen-koo Jeh-neh-reh'eh-tah'ah

136. Tape-to-film

137. Television

138. Test Pattern

139. Title:

  a.   crawl

  b.   roll

  c.   still

  d.   sub-

140. Tonal Proportion

141. Tone

142. Transfer

143. Transistor

144. Transmission

145. Translator

146. Transmitter

136. Teepu Kara Fuirumu
Teh'eh-poo Kah-rah Foo-ee-roo-moo

137. Terebi/Terebijon
Teh-reh-bee/Teh-reh-bee-john

138. Tesuto Pataan
Teh-soo-toh Pah-tah'ahn

139. Taitoru:
Tye-toh-roo:

  a. yukkuri
    yook-koo-ree

  b. ugoku
    oo-goh-koo

  c. seishishita
    say-shee-shee-tah

  d. jimaku
    jee-mah-koo

140. Shikichoo
Shee-kee-choh'oh

141. Shikichoo
Shee-kee-choh'oh

142. Tensoo
Tehn-soh'oh

143. Toranjisutaa
Toh-rahn-jee-soo-tah'ah

144. Sooshin
Soh'oh-sheen

145. Chuukeiki
Choo'oo-kay-kee

146. Sooshinki
Soh'oh-sheen-kee

147. Trichromatic Colors

148. Tuner

149. Tube

150. UHF (ultra-high-frequency)

151. VHF (very-high-frequency)

152. Voltage:

   a.   high

   b.   low

153. Volume

154. Waveform Monitor

155. White Card

Useful Terms:

156. Standby

157. On Air

158. Off Air

147. San Genshoku
     Sahn Gehn-shoh-koo

148. Chuunaa
     Choo'oo-nah'ah

149. Chuubu
     Choo'oo-boo

150. Gokuchoo Tanpa
     Goh-koo-choh'oh Tahn-pah

151. Chootanpa
     Choh'oh-tahn-pah

152. Denatsu:
     Den-ah-tsoo:

   a. takai
       tah-kye

   b. hikui
       hee-koo-ee

153. Boryuumu
     Boh-r'yoo'oo-moo

154. Hakei Monitaa
     Hah-kay Moh-nee-tah'ah

155. Satsueiyoo Howaito Kaado
     Saht-soo-ay-yoh'oh Hoh-wye-toh Kah'ah-doh

Yakunitatsu Kotoba:
Yahk-nee-tah-tsoo Koh-toh-bah:

156. Sutanbai
     Soo-tahn-bye

157. On Eaa
     Ohn Eh-ah'ah

158 Ofu Eaa
     Oh'f Eh-ah'ah

01. Allowance

02. Apprentice

03. Artist

04. Benefits:

  a.   fringe

  b.   health and welfare

  c.   holiday

  d.   pension

  e.   retirement

  f.   vacation

05. Bonus

06. Business Agent

07. Call:

  a.   cancellation of

  b.   change of

01. Teate
    Teh-ah-teh

02. Minarai
    Mee-nah-rye

03. Aachisuto
    Ah'ah-chee-soo-toh

04. Onten:
    Ohn-ten:

  a. kinsengai kyuufu
      keen-sen-gye k''yoo'oo-foo

  b. kenkoo hoken
      ken-koh'oh hoh-ken

  c. kyuujitsu
      k'yoo'oo-jee-tsoo

  d. nenkin
      nen-keen

  e. taishoku
      tye-shoh-koo

  f. kyuuka
      k'yoo'oo-kah

05. Boonasu
    Boh'oh-nah-soo

06. Dairiten
    Dye-ree-ten

07. Seikyuu:
    Say-k'yoo'oo:

  a. kyanseru
      k'yahn-seh-roo

  b. henkoo
      hen-koh'oh

07. Call (continued):

c.   day-

d.   maximum

e.   night-

f.   minimum

08. Callback

09. Check

10. Classification:

a.   higher

b.   lower

11. Conditions

12. Consecutive

13. Craft

14. Crew

15. Crew Member

07. Seikyuu (tsuzuku):
    Say-k'yoo'oo (tsoo-zoo-koo):

  c.   ichinichi atari
        ee-chee-nee-chee ah-tah-ree

  d.   saikoo
        sye-koh'oh

  e.   yakan
        yah-kahn

  f.   saitei
        sye-tay

08. Kitakugo Yobidashi Teate
    Kee-tah-koo-goh Yoh-bee-dah-shee Teh-ah-teh

09. Kogitte
    Koh-geet-teh

10. Bunrui:
    Boon-roo-ee:

  a.   takai
        tah-kye

  b.   hikui
        hee-koo-ee

11. Jooken
    Joh'oh-ken

12. Renzoku
    Ren-zoh-koo

13. Senmonka
    Sehn-mohn-kah

14. Nakama
    Nah-kah-mah

15. Menbaa
    Mehn-bah'ah

16. Cumulative

17. Day Work

18. Deductions

19. Dependent

20. Dismiss

21. Dismissal Time

22. Dismiss For Cause

23. Employee:

a.   daily

b.   female

c.   hourly

d.   male

e.   weekly

f.   staff

24. Employer

16. Ruiseki
    Roo-ee-seh-kee

17. Hiruma no Shigato
    Hee-roo-mah noh Shee-gah-toh

18. Koojo
    Koh'oh-joh

19. Fuyoo Kazoku
    Foo-yoh'oh Kah-zoh-koo

20. Kaiko
    Kye-koh

21. Kaisan Jikoku
    Kye-sahn Jee-koh-koo

22. Kaiko Riyuu
    Kye-koh Ree-yoo'oo

23. Juugyooin:
    Joo'oo-g'yoh'oh-een:

   a. hiyatoi
       hee-yah-toy

   b. josei
       joh-say

   c. jikan gime
       jee-kahn gee-meh

   d. dansei
       dahn-say

   e. shuu yatoi
       shoo'oo yah-toy

   f. shokuin
       shoh-koo-een

24. Koyoosha
    Koh-yoh'oh-shah

25. Employment

26. Experienced

27. Expenses

28. First Unit

29. Freelance

30. Foreman

31. Forelady

32. Grievance

33. Guild

34. Hazard Pay

35. Hire

36. Independent Contractor

37. Insurance

38. Layoff

25. Koyoo
    Koh-yoh'oh

26. Keiken no Aru
    Kay-kehn noh Ah-roo

27. Hiyoo
    Hee-yoh'oh

28. Shuyoo Guruupu
    Shoo-yoh'oh Goo-roo'oo-poo

29. Furiiransaa
    Foo-ree'ee-rahn-sah'ah

30. Shokuchoo
    Shoh-koo-choh'oh

31. Shokuchoo
    Shoh-koo-choh'oh

32. Fuhei Fuman
    Foo-hay Foo-mahn

33. Kumiai
    Koo-mee-eye

34. Kiken Teate
    Kee-kehn Teh-ah-teh

35. Yatou
    Yah-t'ow

36. Dokuritsu Ukeoinin
    Doh-koo-ree-tsoo Oo-keh-oy-neen

37. Hoken
    Hoh-kehn

38. Ichiji Kaiko
    Ee-chee-jee Kye-koh

39. Location:

a.   distant

b.   nearby

40. Lodgings

41. Meal Penalty

42. Meal Period

43. Night Premium

44. Non-union

45. On Call

46. Overnight

47. Pay:

a.   -day

b.   -off

c.   -master

d.   -rate

39. Rokeeshon:
    Roh-keh'eh-shohn:

  a.   tooi
        toh'oh-ee

  b.   chikai
        chee-kye

40. Shukuhaku Shisetsu
    Shoo-koo-hah-koo Shee-seh-tsoo

41. Tokubetsu Teate
    Toh-koo-beh-tsoo Teh-ah-teh

42. Shokuji Jikan
    Shoh-koo-jee Jee-kahn

43. Yakan Warimashi
    Yah-kahn Wah-ree-mah-shee

44. Hi-kumiai
    Hee-koo-mee-eye

45. Irai ni Yotte
    Ee-rye nee Yoht-teh

46. Tetsuya
    Teh-tsoo-yah

47. Kyuuyo:
    K'yoo'oo-yoh:

  a.   -bi
        -bee

  b.   kaiko
        kye-koh

  c.   kaikei gakari
        kye-kay gah-kah-ree

  d.   jikan atari
        jee-kahn ah-tah-ree

48. Per Diem

49. Person

50. Personnel

51. Premium Pay

52. Promotion

53. Quitting Time

54. Rate:

  a.   basic hourly

  b.   daily

  c.   weekly

55. Re-run

56. Residual

57. Rest Period

58. Second Unit

59. Severance

48. Ichinichi Bun
    Ee-chee-nee-chee Boon

49. Hito
    Hee-toh

50. Juugyooin
    Joo'oo-g'yoh'oh-een

51. Warimasi Kyuuyo
    Wah-ree-mah-see K'yoo'oo-yoh

52. Shooshin
    Sho'oh-sheen

53. Shuuryoo Jikoku
    Shoo'oo-r'yoh'oh Jee-koh-koo

54. Kyuuyo/Ryookin:
    K'yoo'oo/R'yoh'oh-keen:

  a.   jikan atari
       jee-kahn ah-tah-ree

  b.   ichinichi atari
       ee-chee-nee-chee ah-tah-ree

  c.   isshuukan atari
       ees-shoo'oo-kahn ah-tah-ree

55. Sai Jooen
    Sye Joh'oh-ehn

56. Zanson
    Zahn-sohn

57. Kyuukei
    K'yoo'oo-kay

58. Yobi Guruupu
    Yoh-bee Goo-roo'oo-poo

59. Maebarai Taishokukin
    Mah-eh-bah-rye Tye-shoh-koo-keen

60. Stand-by

61. Start

62. Start Slip

63. Steward

64. Studio Zone

65. Technician

66. Temporary

67. Time:

a.   -card

b.   double

c.   golden ($2\frac{1}{2}$)

d.   over-

e.   straight

f.   -and-one-half

g.   triple

60. Sutanbai
    Soo-tah-bye

61. Kaishi
    Key-shee

62. Sagyoo-hyoo
    Sah-g'yoh'oh-h'yoh'oh

63. Kujoo Shori Gakari
    Koo-joh'oh Shoh-ree Gah-kah-ree

64. Satsuei Chiiki
    Sah-tsoo-ay Chee'ee-kee

65. Gijutsusha
    Gee-joo-tsoo-shah

66. Rinji no
    Reen-jee noh

67. Jikan:
    Jee-kahn:

   a.   taimu kaado
         tye-moo kah'ah-doh

   b.   baigaku shiharai
         bye-gah-koo shee-hah-rye

   c.   ni ten go bai shiharai
         nee tehn goh bye shee-hah-rye

   d.   zangyoo-
         zahn-g'yoh'oh-

   e.   heijoo
         hay-joh'oh

   f.   i ten go bai shiharai-
         ee tehn goh bye she-hah-rye-

   g.   san bai shiharai
         sahn bye shee-hah-rye

68. Timekeeper

69. Time Worked:

   a.   days

   b.   hours

   c.   months

   d.   weeks

   e.   years

70. Travel Time

71. Union

72. Unemployed

73. Voucher

74. Wages

75. Wrap (quitting time)

68. Keiji Gakari
    Kay-jee Gah-kah-ree

69. Juuji Kikan:
    Joo'oo-jee Kee-kahn:

   a.　nichi
   nee-chee

   b.　jikan
   jee-kahn

   c.　tsuki
   tsoo-kee

   d.　shuu
   shoo'oo

   e.　nen
   nehn

70. Idoo Jikan
    Ee-doh'oh Jee-kahn

71. Roodoo Kumiai
    Roh'oh-doh'oh Koo-mee-eye

72. Shitsugyoosha
    Shee-tsoo-g'yoh'oh-shah

73. Ryooshuusho
    R'yoh'oh-shoo'oo-shoh

74. Kyuuyo
    K'yoo'oo-yoh

75. Shuuryoo Jikan
    Shoo'oo-r'yoh'oh Jee-kahn

01. Can you help me?

02. We wish to film/telecast in/by:

a.   the mountains

b.   the desert

c.   the jungle

d.   a large city

e.   a small village

f.   a river

g.   the street

h.   the road

i.   the outskirts

j.   the beach

k.   a lake

l.   offshore

m.   a remote area

01. O-negai deki-masu ka?
    Oh-neh-gye deh-kee-mah's kah?

02. -- de satsuei shitai
    -- deh sah-tsoo-ay sh't'eye

a.   Yama
     Yah-mah

b.   Sabaku
     Sah-bah-koo

c.   Janguru
     Jahn-goo-roo

d.   Daitoshi
     Dye-toh-shee

e.   Chiisana mura
     Chee'ee-sah-nah moo-rah

f.   Kawa
     Kah-wah

g.   Rojoo
     Roh-joh'oh

h.   Rojoo
     Roh-joh'oh

i.   Koogai
     Koh'oh-gye

j.   Kaigan
     Kye-gahn

k.   Mizuumi
     Mee-zoo-mee

l.   Oki
     Oh-kee

m.   Henpi wa tokoro
     Hehn-pee wah toh-koh-roh

02. We wish to film/telecast in/by (cont):

n.   not too far from civilization

o.   a busy thoroughfare

p.   a quiet street

q.   a residential area

r.   an industrial area

s.   a farm

03. We would like to scout it by:

a.   airplane

b.   boat

c.   car

d.   helicopter

e.   horseback

04. Where can we rent one?

05. Is a map available?

02. -- de satsuei shitai (tsuzuku):
    -- *deh sah-tsoo-ay sh't'eye (tsoo.):*

n.   Inaka
     Ee-nah-kah

o.   Hitodoori no ooi rojoo
     Hee-toh-doh'oh-ree noh oh-oy roh-joh'oh

p.   Shizukana rojoo
     Shee-zoo-kah-nah roh-joh'oh

q.   Juutaku chitai
     Joo'oo-tah-koo chee-tye

r.   Koojoo chitai
     Koh'oh-joh'oh chee-tye

s.   Noojoo
     Noh'oh-joh'oh

03. -- de teisatsu shitai
    -- *deh tay-sah-tsoo sh't'eye*

a.   Hikooki
     Hee-koh'oh-kee

b.   Fune
     Foo-neh

c.   Jidoosha
     Jee-doh'oh-shah

d.   Herikoputaa
     Heh-ree-kohp-tah'ah

e.   Uma ni notte
     Oo-mah nee noht-teh

04. Doko de karire masu ka?
    Doh-koh deh kah-ree-reh mahs kah?

05. Chizu wa arimas ka?
    Chee-zoo wah ah-ree-mahs kah?

06. How much will it cost?

   a.   per day

   b.   per hour

   c.   per week

07. Do we **need** permission to go there?

08. What must we do to

                        get permission?

09. From whom?

10. For each person?

11. Will the permit cover everyone

                        in our group?

12. How long will it take?

   a.   for someone to decide

   b.   to go there and return

13. We want to know ahead of time

06. Ikura desuka?
   Ee-koo-rah dehs'kah

  a.   ichinichi atari
       ee-chee-nee-chee ah-tah-ree

  b.   ichijikan atari
       ee-chee-jee-kahn ah-tah-ree

  c.   isshuukan atari
       ees-shoo'oo-kahn ah-tah-ree

07. Soko e yukunoni kyoka ga irimasu ka?
   Soh-koh eh yoo-koo-noh-nee k'yoh-kah gah
                 ee-ree-mahs kah?

08. Kyoka o torunoni nani o
   K'yoh-kah oh toh-roo-noh-nee nah-nee oh

           shinakereba ikemasenka?
   shee-nah-keh-reh-bah   ee-keh-mah-sehn-kah ?

09. Dare kara desuka?
   Dah-reh kah-rah dehs'kah?

10. Hitori zutsu desuka?
   Hee-toh-ree zoo-tsoo dehs'kah?

11. Kyoka wa guruupu zenin
   K'yoh-kah wah g'roo'oo-poo zen-een

           ni yuukoo desuka?
       nee yoo'oo-koh'oh dehs'kah?

12. -- doregurai no jikan kakarimasu ka?
   -- doh'reh-goo-rye noh jee-kahn kah-kah-ree
                 mahs kah?

  a.   Darekaga kimerunoni
       Dah-reh-kah-gah kee-meh-roo-noh-nee

  b.   Itte Kaerunoni
       Eet-teh Kah-eh-roo-noh-nee

13. Jizan ni shiritai
   Jee-zahn nee shee-ree-tye

14. Must we present our

        documents when we arrive?

15. Who is the person that

                    we contact?

16. Where do we find him/her?

17. Will we need...?

a.   a guide

b.   police escort

c.   military escort

18. We wish to go to...

19. Is it far away?

20. Nearby?

21. Is there a bank there?

22. Is there a public telephone?

23. Are inoculations necessary?

14. Toochaku mei ni shorui o
    Toh'oh-chah-koo mye   nee shoh-roo-ee oh

           misenakereba ikemasen ka?
           mee-seh-nah-keh-reh-bah ee-keh-mah-sehn
                                          kah?

15. Dare ni reraku
    Dah-reh nee reh-rah-koo

              sureba yoi desuka?
              soo-reh-bah yoy dehs'kah?

16. Dokode kare/kanojo ni aimasuka?
    Doh-koh-deh kah-reh/kah-noh-joh nee eye-
                                        mahs'kah?

17. -- ga hitsuyoo desuka?
    -- gah hee-tsoo-yoh'oh dehs'kah?

  a. Gaido
      Gye-doh

  b. Keikan no goei
      Kay-kahn noh goh-ay

  c. Guntai no goei
      Goon-tye noh goh-ay

18. -- e yukitai
    -- eh yoo-kee-tye

19. Tooi desuka?
    Toh-oy dehs'kah?

20. Chikai desuka?
    Chee-kye dehs'kah?

21. Soko ni ginkoo wa arimasuka?
    Soh-koh nee geen-koh'oh wah ah-ree-mahs-
                                        kah?

22. Kooshuu denwa wa arimasuka?
    Koh'oh-shoo'oo den-wah wah ah-ree-mahs'kah?

23. Yoboochuusha wa hitsuyoo desuka?
    Yoh-boh'oh-choo'oo-shah wah hee-tsoo-yoh'oh
                                  dehs'kah?

24. What facilities are available?

a.   film laboratory

b.   television station

c.   equipment rental

d.   caterer

25. Are there experienced personnel?

26. It is very expensive

27. Is everything included?

28. We do not have much time

29. We wish to:

a.   take some photos

b.   take a look at it

c.   see if it will serve

                              our purposes

d.   talk to some people

24. Donna setsubi ga arimasuka?
    Dohn-nah seht-soo-bee gah ah-ree-mahs'kah?

  a.   fuirumu genzoojo
       foo-ee-roo-moo gehn-zoh'oh-joh

  b.   terebi kyoku
       teh-reh-bee k'yoh-koo

  c.   kizai no rentaru
       Kee-zye noh rehn-tah-roo

  d.   makanai nin
       mah-kah-nye neen

25. Keikensha wa imasuka?
    Kay-kehn-shah wah ee-mahs'kah?

26. Hijooni takai desuka?
    Hee-joh'oh-nee tah-kye dehs'kah?

27. Subete fukumarete imasuka?
    Soo-beh-teh foo-koo-mah-reh-teh ee-mahs'ka?

28. Sonnani jikan ga nai
    Sohn-nah-nee jee-kahn gah nye

29. -- shitai
    -- sh'tye

  a.   Shashin o toritai
       Shah-sheen oh toh-ree-tye

  b.   Mitemitai
       Mee-teh-mee-tye

  c.   Mokuteki ni au ka
       Moh-k'teh-kee nee ow kah

                       dooka mitemitai
             doh'oh-kah mee-teh-mee-tye

  d.   Dareka ni hanashi o
       Dah-reh-kah nee hah-nah-shee oh

29. We wish to (continued):

e.   see a certain person

f.   employ people

g.   hire animals

h.   rent equipment

30. We will need accomodations:

a.   food

b.   a good restaurant

c.   lodgings

d.   single

e.   double

f.   suite

g.   with bath

h.   air conditioning

i.   quiet

29. -- shitai (tsuzuku):
    -- sh'tye (tsoo-zoo-koo):

e.   Hitoni aitai
     Hee-toh-nee eye-tye

f.   Hito o yatoitai
     Hee-toh oh yah-toy-tye

g.   Doobutsu o karitai
     Doh'oh-boo-tsoo oh kah-ree-tye

h.   Kizai o karitai
     Kee-zye oh kah-ree-tye

30. -- no setsubi ga hitsuyoodesu
    -- noh seht-soo-bee gah hee-tsoo-yoh'oh-
                                          dehs

a.   Shokuji
     Shoh-koo-jee

b.   Yoi resutoran
     Yoy reh-soo-toh-rahn

c.   Yado
     Yah-doh

d.   Shinguru no heya
     Sheen-goo-roo noh heh-yah

e.   Daburu no heya
     Dah-boo-roo noh heh-yah

f.   Suiito
     Soo-ee-toh

g.   Furotsuki no heya
     Foo-roh-tsoo-kee no heh-yah

h.   Eakontsuki no heya
     Eh-ah-kohn-tsoo-kee noh heh-yah

i.   Shizukana heya
     Shee-zoo-kah-nah heh-yah

30. We will need accomodations (cont):

j.   tent

k.   camping gear

l.   beer

m.   whiskey

31. If we dislike something

we are annoyed

32. You are very kind

33. We will be in that

location   for:

a.   days

b.   weeks

c.   months

d.   a short time

e.   a long time

30. -- no setsubi ga hitsuyoodesu (tsuzuku):
    -- noh seht-soo-bee gah hee-tsoo-yoh'oh-
    dehs (tsoo.)

 j. Tento
     Tehn-toh

 k. Kyanpu yoohin
     K'yahn-poo yoh'oh-heen

 l. Biiru
     Bee'ee-roo

 m. Uisukii
     Oo-ee-s'kee'ee

31. Ki ni iranai koto ga
    Kee nee ee-rah-nye koh-toh gah

                       aruto nayamasaremasu
          ah-roo-toh nah-yah-mah-sah-reh-mahs

32. Goshinsetsu arigatoo
    Goh-sheen-seh-tsoo ah-ree-gah-toh'oh

33. Sono basho ni --
    Soh-noh bah-shoh nee --

                               imasu:
                             ee-mah-soo:

 a. nichi
     nee-chee

 b. shuu
     shoo'oo

 c. tsuki
     tsoo-kee

 d. tankikan
     tahn-kee-kahn

 e. chookikan
     choh'oh-kee-kahn

34. We will transport the crew by:

a.   bus

b.   plane

c.   train

d.   car

e.   wagon

f.   ship

g.   boat

35. Wear:

a.   light clothing

b.   winter clothing

c.   boots

d.   raingear

e.   sun hat

f.   gloves

34. Kuruu o -- de okurimasu:
    Koo-roo'oo oh -- deh oh-koo-ree-mahs:

a.   basu
      bah-soo

b.   hikooki
      hee-koh'oh-kee

c.   kisha
      kee-shah

d.   kuruma
      koo-roo-mah

e.   basha
      bah-shah

f.   fune
      foo-neh

g.   booto
      boh'oh-toh

35. Fukusoo:
    Foo-koo-soh'oh:

a.   Keikaina-
      Kay-kye-nah-

b.   Fuyu yoo no-
      Foo-yoo yoh'oh noh-

c.   buutsu
      bou'oo-tsoo

d.   amagu
      ah-mah-goo

e.   booshi
      boh'oh-shee

f.   tebukuro
      teh-boo-koo-roh

36. Beware of:

a.   snakes

b.   reptiles

c.   insects

d.   wild animals

37. Take insect repellant

38. We will arrive at our destination:

a.   on time

b.   late

c.   early

39. Where can I cash

                    traveler's checks?

40. Where can I exchange my

            country's currency for yours?

36. -- ni kio tsukero:
    -- nee kee-oh tsoo-keh-roh:

 a.   Hebi
      Heh-bee

 b.   Hachuurui
      Hah-choo'oo-roo-ee

 c.   Mushi
      Moo-shee

 d.   Yasei doobutsu
      Yah-say doh'oh-boo-tsoo

37. Sacchuuzai o motte ike
    Saht-choo'oo-zye oh moht-teh ee-keh

38. Mokutekichi ni -- toochakusuru:
    Moh-koo-teh-kee-chee nee -- toh'oh-chah-
    *   koo-s'roo*

 a.   teikoku doori
      tay-koh-koo doh'oh-ree

 b.   okurete
      oh-koo-reh-teh

 c.   hayaku
      hah-yah-koo

39. Dokode toraberaazu chekku
    Doh-koh-deh toh-rah-beh-rah'ah-zoo chehk-
    *   koo*

              o genkin ni dekimasuka?
         oh gehn-keen nee deh-kee-mahs'kah?

40. Dokode genchi tsuuka ni
    Doh-koh-deh gehn-chee tsoo-kah'ah nee

              ryoogae dekimasuka?
         r'yoh'oh-gah-eh deh-kee-mahs'kah?

41. What is the rate of

                             exchange today?

42. At least one room on the ground

                        floor for the equipment

43. We have arrived

44. This is the place

45. We must leave

46. This will not do

47. We will go elsewhere

48. How much will this cost?

49. Too expensive

50. Inexpensive

51. There is an extra charge

                                        for that

52. Is that clear?

41. Kyoo no kookan reeto wa
    K'yoh'oh noh koh'oh-kahn reh'eh-toh wah

                        ikura desuka?
                        ee-koo-rah dehs'kah?

42. Sukunakutomo ikkaino
    Soo-koo-nah-koo-toh-moh eek-kye-noh

                    hitoheya wa kizaiyoo desu
         hee-toh-heh-yah wah kee-zye-oh'oh   dehs

43. Toochaku shimishita
    Toh'oh-chah-koo shee-mee-shee-tah

44. Koko ga sono basho desu
    Koh-koh gah soh-noh bah-shoh dehs

45. Ikanakereba narimasen
    Ee-kah-nah-keh-reh-bah nah-ree-mah-sehn

46. Korewa yokunai
    Koh-reh-wah yoh-koo-nye

47. Dokoka hoka e ikimasu
    Doh-koh-kah hoh-kah eh ee-kee-mahs

48. Ikura kakarimasuka?
    Ee-koo-rah kah-kah-ree-mahs'kah?

49. Takasugiri
    Tah-kah-soo-gee-ree

50. Yasui
    Yah-soo-ee

51. Yobuno hiyoo ga
    Yoh-boo-noh hee-yoh'oh gah

                        kakarimasu
                        kah-kah-ree-mahs

52. Sore wa kirei desuka?
    Soh-reh wah kee-ray dehs'ka?

53. That is my final offer

54. We do not spend money

                          foolishly

55. This is a business venture

56. We are not tourists, we

                      are here to work

57. What did you say?

58. I must have your answer now

59. I haven't much time

60. Think about it

61. Exactly

62. Agreed

63. Location work is difficult

64. It requires attention to

                          details

53. Kore ga saigo no teiji desu
    Koh-reh gah sye'goh noh tay-jee dehs

54. Watakushitachi wa sonna bakana
    Wah-tah-koo-shee-tah-chee wah sohn-nah bah-
    *   kah-nah*

    kane no tsukaikata wa shimasen
    kah-neh noh tsoo-kye-kah-tah wah shee-mah-
    *   sehn*

55. Kore wa shigotojoo no kane desu
    Koh-reh wah shee-goh-toh-joh'oh noh kah-neh
    *   dehs*

56. Asobi dewa naku
    Ah-soh-bee deh-wah nah-koo

                shigoto ni kiteimasu
    shee-goh-toh nee kee-tay-mahs

57. Nanto iimashitaka?
    Nahn-toh ee'ee-mah-shee-tah-kah?

58. Ima henji ga moraitai
    Ee-mah hehn-jee gah moh-rye-tye

59. Amari jikan ga nai
    Ah-mah-ree jee-kahn gah nye

60. Kangaete oite kudasai
    Kahn-gah-eh-teh oy-teh koo-dah-sye

61. Sono toori
    Soh-noh toh'oh-ree

62. Dooi shimasu
    Doh-oy shee-mahs

63. Rokeishohn wa muzukashii
    Roh-kay-shohn wah moo-zoo-kah-shee'ee

64. Komakai chuui ga hitsuyoo desu
    Koh-mah-kye choo'oo-ee gah hee-tsoo-yoh'oh
    *   dehs*

01. Name of consignor (shipper)

02. Name of consignee (receiver)

03. Last name

04. First name

05. Address

06. Via:

a.   air

b.   ship

c.   train

d.   truck

07. Is the address on each case?

08. What carrier?

09. I shall carry this myself

10. Here is:

a.   my passport

ZAY-KAHN

01. Shukka nin
    Shoo'k-kah neen

02. Niuke nin
    Nee-oo-keh neen

03. Myooji
    M'yoh'oh-jee

04. Namae
    Nah-mah-eh

05. Juusho
    Joo'oo-shoh

06. -- bin:
    -- been:

   a.   Kooku
         Koh'oh-koo

   b.   Funa
         Foo-nah

   c.   Ressha
         Rehs-shah

   d.   Torakku
         Toh-rahk-koo

07. Dono hakonimo juusho ga arimasuka?
    Doh-noh hah-koh-nee-moh joo'oo-shoh gah
    ah-ree-mahs kah?

08. Unsoo gyoosha wa?
    Oon-soh'oh g'yoh'oh-shah wah?

09. Jibunde hakobimasu
    Jee-boon-deh hah-koh-bee-mahs

10. Korega watakushi no -- desu
    Koh-reh-gah wah-tah-koo-shee noh -- dehs

   a.   pasupooto
         pahs'poh'oh-toh

10. Here is (continued):

b.   my identification

c.   my visa

d.   my work permit

e.   my airbill

f.   my waybill

g.   my equipment list

11. Here are the baggage checks

12. I have _____ pieces

of equipment and _____

pieces of personal luggage

13. That is not mine

14. That one is mine

15. One item is missing

16. Check with lost and found

10. Korega watakushi no -- desu (tsu.)
    Koh-reh-gah wah-tah-koo-shee noh -- dehs
    (tsoo.)

 b. mibun shoomeisho
    mee-boon shoh'oh-may-shoh

 c. biza
    bee-zah

 d. roodoo kyokasho
    roh'oh-doh'oh k'yoh-kah-shoh

 e. kookuu kamotsu okurijoo
    koh'oh-koo'oo kah-moh-tsoo oh-koo-ree-
    joh'oh

 f. kamotsu okurijoo
    kah-moh-tsoo oh-koo-ree-joh'oh

 g. kizai risuto
    kee-zye ree-soo-toh

11. Korega nimotsuken desu
    Koh-reh-gah nee-moh-tsoo-kehn dehs

12. Kizai ga -- ko to
    Kee-zye gah -- koh toh

                    minomawarihin ga
          mee-noh-mah-wah-ree-heen gah

                         -- ko desu
                         -- koh dehs

13. Korewa watakushino monodewa nai
    Koh-reh-wah wah-tah-koo-shee-noh moh-noh-
    deh-wah nye

14. Korewa watakushino mono desu
    Koh-reh-wah wah-tah-koo-shee-no moh-noh
    dehs

15. Ikko funshitsu shiteimasu
    Eek-koh foon-sh'tsoo shee-tay-mah-soo

16. Ishitsubutsu gakari de shirabete
    Ee-shee-tsoo-boo-tsoo gah-kah-ree deh shee-
    rah-beh-teh

17. Must we open each case?

18. I have nothing to declare

19. Regulations are regulations

20. Can we hasten this someway?

21. It is against regulations

22. This is all I have to declare

23. This cannot be opened

                                    for inspection

24. Why not?

25. It will be ruined if exposed

                                    to light

26. But it must be inspected

27. I cannot permit it

28. Then it cannot go through

29. Who is in charge here?

17. Ikko zutsu akeruno desuka?
    Eek-koh zoo-tsoo ah-keh-roo-noh dehs'kah?

18. Shinkoku suru mono wa arimasen
    Sheen-koh-koo soo-roo moh-noh wah ah-ree-
    mah-sehn

19. Kisoku wa kisoku desu
    Kee-soh-koo wah kee-soh-koo dehs

20. Nanika isogu hoohoo wa arimasuka?
    Nah-nee-kah ee-soh-goo hoh'oh-hoh'oh wah
    ah-ree-mahs'kah?

21. Sore wa kisokuihan desu
    Soh-reh wah kee-soh-koo-ee-hahn dehs

22. Korega shinkokusuru monono subete desu
    Koh-reh-gah sheen-koh-koo-soo-roo moh-noh
    s'beh-teh dehs

23. Kensa no tame ni
    Kehn-sah noh tah-meh nee

                       akerukoto wa dekimasen
          ah-keh-roo-koh-toh wah deh-kee-mah-sehn

24. Naze desuka?
    Nah-zeh dehs'kah?

25. Hikari ni ataruto
    Hee-kah-ree nee ah-tah-roo-toh

                       dame ni nari masu
                dah-meh nee nah-ree mahs

26. Demo kensa shinakereba narimasen
    Deh-moh kehn-sah shee-nah-keh-reh-bah nah-
    ree-mah-sehn

27. Kyoka dekimasen
    K'yoh-kah deh-kee-mah-sehn

28. Soredewa tsuukan dekimasen
    Soh-reh-deh-wah tsoo'oo-kahn deh-kee-mah-
    sehn

29. Kokona tantoosha wa dare desuka?
    Koh-koh-nah tahn-toh'oh-shah wah dah-reh
    dehs'kah?

30. What is his name?

31. I would like to see him

32. What is your name?

33. How long will it take?

34. We registered the equipment

                          before we left

35. The rawstock also

36. We will purchase rawstock

                    here and send it home

                after it has been exposed

37. We will pay duty on it

38. The name of the custom

                          broker is ____

39. I have a registry receipt

                for the equipment and rawstock

30. Sonohito no namae wa nan desuka?
    Soh-noh-hee-toh noh nah-mah-eh wah nahn
                                          dehs'kah?

31. Sonohito ni aitai
    Soh-noh-hee-toh nee eye-tye

32. Anata no namae wa nan desuka?
    Ah-nah-tah noh nah-mah-eh wah nahn dehs'kah?

33. Doregurai kakarimasuka?
    Doh-reh-goo-rye kah-kah-ree-mahs'kah?

34. Shuppatsu mae ni kizai
    Shoop-pah-tsoo mah-eh nee kee-zye

                    no tooroku o shimashita
          noh toh'oh-roh-koo oh shee-mah-sh'tah

35. Fuirumu no desu
    Foo-ee-roo-moo noh dehs

36. Fuirumu wa kochira de
    Foo-ee-roo-moo wah koh-chee-rah deh

                    kaimotome satsueigo
          kye-moh-toh-meh sah-tsoo-ay-goh

                    mochi kaeri masu
          moh-chee kah-eh-ree mahs

37. Koreno kanzei o haraimasu
    Koh-reh-noh kahn-zay oh hah-rye-mah-soo

38. Tsuukan gyoosha no
    Tsoo'oo-kahn g'yoh'oh-shah noh

                    namae wa -- desu
          nah-mah-eh wah -- dehs

39. Kizai to fuirumu noh toorokusho
    Kee-zye toh foo-ee-roo-moo noh toh'oh-roh-
                                      koo-shoh
                    noh uketori o motteimasu
          noh oo-keh-toh-ree oh moht-tay-mahs

40. Here is the manifest

41. Each item is listed with:

a.   a serial number and weight

b.   the country where it was manufactured

42. When we ship,

                        we always notify

                        our customs broker

43. We also send the

                        airbill/waybill number

                        and announce when the

                        shipment is due to arrive

44. We also attach all

                        the numbers of the

                        airbill/waybill

                        to each case

40. Korega ichiranhyoo desu
    Koh-reh-gah ee-chee-rahn-h'yoh'oh dehs

41. Kono risuto wa -- o fukumu
    Koh-noh ree-soo-toh wah -- oh foo-koo-moo

  a.   bangoo to juuryoo betsu
    bahn-goh'oh toh joo'oo-r'yoh'oh beh-tsoo

  b.   seizoo koojoo betsu
    say-zoh'oh koh'oh-joh'oh beh-tsoo

42. Itsumo shukka suru
    Ee-tsoo-moh shoo'k-kah soo-roo

              toki wa tsuukangyoosha
    toh-kee wah tsoo'oo-kahn-g'yoh-oh-shah

                ni renraku shimasu
    nee rehn-rah-koo sh'mahs

43. Shoruibangoo mo tsutae
    Shoh-roo-ee-bahn-goh'oh moh tsoo-tah-eh

                  mata nimotsu
    mah-tah nee-moh-tsoo

                toochaku yoteibi
    toh'oh-chah'k yoh-tay-bee

                o renraku shimasu
    oh rehn-rah-koo sh'mahs

44. Mata sorezoreno
    Mah-tah soh-reh-zoh-reh-noh

                hako ni-shorui
    hah-koh nee shoh-roo-ee

                  bangoo o
    bahn-goh'oh oh

                  tsukemasu
    tsoo-keh-mahs

45. The customs broker charges

a service fee

for each shipment

46. Don't forget to add

freight fee charged

by the carrier

47. In some countries,

one has to pay additional

tax for

exposed film upon

leaving

48. Often there is a delivery

charge for film between

point of entry

and the laboratory

45. Tsuukan gyoosha wa shukka
    Tsoo'oo-kahn g'yoh'oh-shah wah shoo'k-kah

                    gotoni tesuuryoo o
        goh-toh-nee teh-soo'oo-r'yoh'oh oh

                        seikyuu shimasu
            say-k'yoo'oo shee-mah-soo

46. Unsoogyoosha ni yotte
    Oon-soh'oh-g'yoh'oh-shah nee yoht-teh

                unchin ga kasan sareru koto
        oon-cheen gah kah-sahn sah-reh-roo koh-toh

                    o wasuretewa ikemasen
            oh wah-s'reh-teh-wah ee-keh-mah-sen

47. Aru kuni dewa
    Ah-roo koo-nee deh-wah

                    satsueizumi fuirumu ni
        sah-tsoo-ay-zoo-mee foo-ee-roo-moo nee

                        yobun no
                    yoh-boon noh

                    tsuukanryoo ga
            tsoo'oo-kahn-r'yoh'oh gah

                        hitsuyoo desu
                hee-tsoo-yoh'oh dehs

48. Minato kara genzoojo madeno
    Mee-nah-toh kah-rah gehn-zoh'oh-joh mah-den
                                            -oh

                    fuirumu haitatsuryoo
        foo-ee-roo-moo hye-tah-tsoo-r'yoh'oh

                        ga seikyuu
                    gah say-k'yoo'oo

                    sareru koto ga arimasu
            sah-reh-roo koh-toh gah ah-ree-mahs

49. Is this equipment

                        being imported?

50. Not at all

51. It is being brought in for

                        use on a production

52. Then, we will take it back

53. If that is not stated

                        you will have to pay

                        an import tax

54. How can we get this through

                        customs quickly?

55. Be sure to get your papers

                        stamped: Passed

56. Never try to smuggle anything

                        in or out

49. Kono kizai wa yunyuu
    Koh-noh kee-zye wah yoo-n'yoo'oo

                        sarete imasuka?
                        sah-reh-teh ee-mah-s'kah ?

50. Zenzen sarete imasen
    Zen-zen sah-reh-teh ee-mah-sehn

51. Korewa produkushon yooni
    Koh-reh-wah proh-doo-koo-shohn yoh'oh-nee

                        mochikaeri mashita
                        moh-chee-kah-eh-ree mah-sh'tah

52. Dewa sore o mochikerimasu
    Deh-wah soh-reh oh moh-chee-keh-ree-mahs

53. Moshi sore o meikishite nakereba
    *Moh-shee soh-reh oh may-kee-sh'teh nah-
                                keh-reh-bah*

                        yunyuuzei o shiharawa
                        yoo-n'yoo'oo-zay oh shee-hah-rah-wah

                        nakereba narimasen
                        nah-keh-reh-bah nah-ree-mah-sehn

54. Hayaku tsuukan suru niwa
    Hah-yah-koo tsoo'oo-kahn soo-roo nee-wah

                        dooshitara yoi deshooka?
                        doh'oh-sh'tah-rah yoy deh-shoh'oh-kah?

55. Kanarazu shorui ni "SHOONIN"
    *Kah-nah-rah-zoo shoh-roo-ee nee "SHOH'OH
                                        -NEEN"*

                        in o oshite kudasai
                        een oh oh-sh'teh koo-dah-sye

56. Zettaini mitsuyu shiyoo
    Zeht-tye-nee mee-tsoo-yoo shee-yoh'oh

                        to shitewa ikemasen
                        toh sh'teh-wah ee-keh-mah-sen

Useful Terms:

57. Enter

58. Exit

59. Customs Inspection

60. Customs Broker

61. Carrier

62. Freight Pickup and Receiving

63. Passport Office

64. Immigration

ZAY-KAHN (tsoo-zoo-koo)

Yakunitatsu Kotoba:
Yahk-nee-tah-tsoo Koh-toh-bah:

57. Iriguchi
    Ee-ree-goo-chee

58. Deguchi
    Deh-goo-chee

59. Zeikan
    Zay-kahn

60. Tsuukangyoosha
    Tsoo'oo-kahn-g'yoh'oh-shah

61. Unsoo Gyoosha
    Oon-soh'oh G'yoh'oh-shah

62. Kamotsu Hikitori Uketsuke
    Kah-moh-tsoo Hee-kee-toh-ree Oo-keh-tsoo-
    keh

63. Ryoken Jimusho
    R'yoh-kehn Jee-moo-shoh

64. Nyuugoku Kanri
    N'yoo'oo-goh-koo Kahn-ree

Time:

01. Year

02. Month

   a.   January

   b.   February

   c.   March

   d.   April

   e.   May

   f.   June

   g.   July

   h.   August

   i.   September

   j.   October

   k.   November

   l.   December

Jikan:
Jee-kahn:

01. Toshi
    Toh-shee

02. Tsuki/Gatsu
    Tsoo-kee/Gah-tsoo

 a.   Ichi-gatsu
       Ee-chee-gah-tsoo

 b.   Ni-gatsu
       Nee-gah-tsoo

 c.   San-gatsu
       Sahn-gah-tsoo

 d.   Shi-gatsu
       Shee-gah-tsoo

 e.   Go-gatsu
       Goh-gah-tsoo

 f.   Roku-gatsu
       Roh-koo-gah-tsoo

 g.   Shichi-gatsu
       Shee-chee-gah-tsoo

 h.   Hachi-gatsu
       Hah-chee-gah-tsoo

 i.   Ku-gatsu
       Koo-gah-tsoo

 j.   Juu-gatsu
       Joo'oo-gah-tsoo

 k.   Juuichi-gatsu
       Joo'oo-ee-chee-gah-tsoo

 i.   Juuni-gatsu
       Joo'oo-nee-gah-tsoo

Time (continued):

03. Week:

a. Monday

b. Tuesday

c. Wednesday

d. Thursday

e. Friday

f. Saturday/Sunday

04. Day

05. Hour

06. Minute

07. Second

08. Dawn

09. Morning

10. Noon

Jikan (tsuzuku):
Jee-kahn (tsoo-zoo-koo):

03. Shuu:
    Shoo'oo:

  a.   Getsu-yoobi
       Geh-tsoo-yoh'oh-bee

  b.   Ka-yoobi
       Kah-yoh'oh-bee

  c.   Sui-yoobi
       Soo-ee-yoh'oh-bee

  d.   Moku-yoobi
       Moh-koo-yoh'oh-bee

  e.   Kin-yoobi
       Keen-yoh'oh-bee

  f.   Do-yoobi/Nichi-yoobi
       Doh-yoh'oh-bee/Nee-chee-yoh'oh-bee

04. Hi
    Hee

05. Jikan
    Jee-kahn

06. Fun
    Foon

07. Byoo
    B'yoh'oh

08. Yoake
    Yoh-ah-keh

09. Asa
    Ah-sah

10. Hiru/Shoogo
    Hee-roo/Shoh'oh-goh

<u>Time (continued)</u>:

11. Afternoon

12. Dusk

13. Night

14. Midnight

15. A.M.

16. P.M.

17. Early

18. Late

19. On Time

20. Today

21. Tomorrow

22. Yesterday

23. Day after tomorrow

24. Day before yesterday

JIKAN (tsuzuku):
Jee-kahn (tsoo-zoo-koo):

11. Gogo
    Goh-goh

12. Hakubo
    Hah-koo-boh

13. Yoru
    Yoh-roo

14. Yonaka
    Yoh-nah-kah

15. Gozen
    Goh-zen

16. Gogo
    Goh-goh

17. Hayai
    Hah-y'eye

18. Osoi
    Oh-soy

19. Teikoku Doori
    Tay-kah-koo Doh'oh-ree

20. Kyoo
    K'yoh'oh

21. Asu
    Ah-soo

22. Kinoo
    Kee-noh'oh

23. Asatte
    Ah-saht-teh

24. Ototsui
    Oh-toh-tsoo-ee

Numbers:

25. One

26. Two

27. Three

28. Four

29. Five

30. Six

31. Seven

32. Eight

33. Nine

34. Ten

35. Eleven

36. Twelve

37. Thirteen

38. Fourteen

Kazu:
Kah-zoo:

25. Ichi
    Ee-chee

26. Ni
    Nee

27. San
    Sahn

28. Shi/Yon
    Shee/Yohn

29. Go
    Goh

30. Roku
    Roh-koo

31. Shichi/Nana
    Shee-chee/Nah-nah

32. Hachi
    Hah-chee

33. Kyuu/Ku
    K'yoo/Koo

34. Juu
    Joo'oo

35. Juuichi
    Joo'oo-ee-chee

36. Juuni
    Joo'oo-nee

37. Juusan
    Joo'oo-sahn

38. Juushi/Juuyon
    Joo'oo-shee/Joo'oo-yohn

Numbers (continued):

39. Fifteen

40. Twenty

41. Thirty

42. Forty

43. Fifty

44. Sixty

45. Seventy

46. Eighty

47. Ninety

48. Hundred

49. Thousand

50. Million

51. Billion

52. Trillion

Kazu (tsuzuku):
Kah-zoo (tsoo-zoo-koo):

39. Juugo
    Joo'oo-goh

40. Nijuu
    Nee-joo'oo

41. Sanjuu
    Sahn-joo'oo

42. Yonjuu/Shijuu
    Yoh-joo'oo/Shee-joo'oo

43. Gojuu
    Goh-joo'oo

44. Rokujuu
    Roh-koo-joo'oo

45. Shichijuu/Nanajuu
    Shee-chee-joo'oo/Nah-nah-joo'oo

46. Hachijuu
    Hah-chee-joo'oo

47. Kyuujuu
    K'yoo'oo-joo'oo

48. Hyaku
    H'yah-koo

49. Sen
    Sehn

50. Hyakuman
    H'yahk'mahn

51. Juuoku
    Joo'oo-oh-koo

52. Icchoo
    Eet-choh'oh

Math:

53. Add

54. Subtract

55. Divide

56. Multiply

57. Circle

58. Square

59. Rectangle

60. Circumference

61. Diameter

62. Segment

63. Half

64. Quarter

65. Three-quarters

Suugaku:
Soo'oo-gah-koo:

53. Tasu
    Tah-soo

54. Hiku
    Hee-koo

55. Waru
    Wah-roo

56. Kakeru
    Kah-keh-roo

57. En
    Ehn

58. Seihookei
    Say-hoh'oh-kay

59. Choohookei
    Choh'oh-hoh'oh-kay

60. Enshuu
    Ehn-shoo'oo

61. Chokkei
    Chohk-kay

62. Kubun/Segumento
    Koo-boon/Sehg'mehn-toh

63. Ni Bun No Ichi
    Nee Boon Noh Ee-chee

64. Yon Bun No Ichi
    Yohn Boon Noh Ee-chee

65. Yon Bun No San
    Yohn Boon Noh Ee-chee

Weather:

66. Clear

67. Cloudy

68. Cold

69. Fog

70. Hail

71. Hot

72. Humid

73. Overcast

74. Rain

75. Sleet

76. Snow

77. Sunny

78. Variable

79. Windy

Tenkoo:
Tehn-koh'oh:

66. Hare
    Hah-reh

67. Kumori
    Koo-moh-ree

68. Samui
    Sah-moo-ee

69. Kiri
    Kee-ree

70. Arare
    Ah-rah-reh

71. Atsui
    Aht-soo-ee

72. Mushi Atsui
    Moo-shee Aht-soo-ee

73. Kumori
    Koo-moh-ree

74. Ame
    Ah-meh

75. Mizore
    Mee-zoh-reh

76. Yuki
    Yoo-kee

77. Seiten
    Say-tehn

78. Tokidoki
    Toh-kee-doh-kee

79. Kaze
    Kah-zeh

ADDITIONAL TERMS

ADDITIONAL TERMS

SECTION   PAGE   TERM

ADDITIONAL TERMS

SECTION	AGE	TERM

ADDITIONAL TERMS

SECTION	PAGE	TERM

ADDITIONAL TERMS

ADDITIONAL TERMS

SECTION   PAGE   TERM

Translation
of
FILM & VIDEO
TERMS

Compiled by
Verne Carlson

English translated into
SPANISH • FRENCH • GERMAN
ITALIAN • JAPANESE

A boxed set of 5 books that is a must for
those engaged in production work. Each
book contains more than 2500 motion picture
and TV terms used by American and English-
speaking crews operating world-wide. The
vocabulary covers camera, editing, lighting,
grip, sound & script, as well as personnel,
video, production, tools, and getting through
customs. This erases many problems and
misunderstandings inherent when filming
overseas.

A Miscellaneous section covers Time,
Numbers, Math and Weather.

NEED MORE BOOKS?
order from

YOUR BOOKSELLER, or
DOUBLE C Publishing Company
120 East Verdugo Avenue
Burbank, California 91502

Please Reserve:

Set of FIVE...OR individual volume of
French......German......Italian......
Spanish.....Japanese......

Name(Print)...........................
Address...............................
City..................................
State.......................Zip.......
I enclose check/International Money
order for $...........................

Translation
of
FILM & VIDEO
TERMS

**Compiled by
Verne Carlson**

English translated into
SPANISH • FRENCH • GERMAN
ITALIAN • JAPANESE

A boxed set of 5 books that is a must for those engaged in production work. Each book contains more than 2500 motion picture and TV terms used by American and English-speaking crews operating world-wide. The vocabulary covers camera, editing, lighting, grip, sound & script, as well as personnel, video, production, tools, and getting through customs. This erases many problems and misunderstandings inherent when filming overseas.

A Miscellaneous section covers Time, Numbers, Math and Weather.

NEED MORE BOOKS?
order from

YOUR BOOKSELLER, or
DOUBLE C Publishing Company
120 East Verdugo Avenue
Burbank, California 91502

Please Reserve:

Set of FIVE...OR individual volume of
French......German......Italian......
Spanish.....Japanese......

Name(Print)........................
Address............................
City...............................
State.....................Zip.......
I enclose check/International Money
order for $........................